Self Suffic

Self Sufficiency Co

For Beginners

Nancy Ross

Table of Contents

Book 1: Tiny Houses

Book 2: Backyard Chickens

Book 3: Homesteading

Book 4: Mini Farming

Tiny Houses
A Beginners Guide To Tiny House Living
Nancy Ross

Table of Contents

Introduction

Chapter 1: The Tiny Home Movement

Chapter 2: Financing Your Tiny Home

Chapter 3: Location and Building Your Tiny Home

Chapter 4: Easy Space Hacks to Make Tiny Home Living Easier

Chapter 5: Living Room

Chapter 6: Bathroom

Chapter 7: Bedrooms

Chapter 8: Tips and Tricks to Understand Tiny Home Living

Conclusion

Introduction

The tiny home movement has taken the world by storm. In the wake of the current housing industry getting incredibly hard to deal with, with high prices and houses that are too big for most people to deal with, and the fact that most people are hard on the environment with their housing choices, many people are starting to turn to a new solution. And that solution is tiny homes.

Tiny homes are a great idea to make some changes. These homes come in under 400 square feet, making just enough room for you to have yourself and a few other people. With the average American home over 2000 square feet, this is quite a bit smaller than what most people are used to. But the idea is to just use the amount of space that is needed while saving money on the home and even your utilities.

Moving into a tiny home is not always the easiest thing to do. We are used to have a lot of space and most of us would have no idea of how to live in such limited space. But with the help of this guidebook, you will learn how great the tiny home movement can be and some of the best tips that you can follow to make living in this kind of home as easy as possible.

Whether you are just starting out on your journey and looking into how tiny homes work or you have been on this path for some time and are ready to jump in, this guidebook is going to have all the information that you need to get started on the right foot. Read through this guidebook and get all the information you need to start living the tiny home movement!

Chapter 1: The Tiny Home Movement

Many Americans dream of owning their own house someday. They may have dreams of going for one of the biggest homes that they can find, choosing to go as far as their budge can fly. This is the American dream, to be able to keep up with the Jones's and really enjoy life. It has been the way for years and the fact that there are millions of huge homes all across the country is a testament to this fact.

But there is a growing trend that is going the other way. Some people are seeing the folly of owning such a big home. Most people do not need that much room and the waste of all the materials, utilities, and overall cost of these homes can be outrageous. Add on the fact that the housing market rates keep going up, and you either end up with a mortgage you just can't afford or a house that is just too big to handle.

The tiny home movement is taking things the other way. People are tired of the waste, realize that they don't need that much space, or they want an affordable way to be able to move into their first home. This movement asks you to step back rom those big mansions that are not worth the hassle, and instead move into a tiny little home that is just big enough for your belongings and nothing else.

It can be kind of hard to imagine. The tiny home movement is asking you to move all of your family and your belongings into a tiny space, usually no bigger than a medium sized hotel room overall. Think of it, you are going to have to stuff all your things into a tiny area, including the bathroom, kitchen, living room, and any bedrooms.

Now, there are some adjustments that can be made to the tiny home and still fit in. A family of ten is probably not going to fit into a true tiny home that is 400 square feet or under. But the main idea of the tiny home movement is to get rid of waste and only use the space that you need. If you're a family of ten, you can still be a part of this movement if you pick a house that is slightly bigger, but opt out of the big mansion style home.

Deciding on the Tiny Home Movement

There are many people who are choosing to go with the tiny home movement. It is a great way to be good to the environment, to learn how to be careful with our actions, and to even find a home that is pretty affordable.

Basically, the tiny home movement can be split up into two groups. A tiny home is any that is 400 square feet and under. This isn't very much space though and there are many families who would like to join in on the movement, but the space is just a little too limited. The second group is the small house movement. This provides a bit more space, up to 1000 square feet, but is still much smaller than you will find with many of the other homes on the market.

Either way that you choose, the tiny home movement is meant to help you be more conscientious with your decisions. It is for the person who is tired of all the waste that is going on around them and wants a chance to be good to the environment. It is for the person who wants to save money and not have to worry about a lot of space or coming up with the utility bill. It is for that person who feels that the huge houses are just wasteful and realizes they just need a place to eat and lay their heads when it is time for bed. It is even for the person who has been saving for their first house, but who feels that they will never reach this goal.

The tiny home movement is not just about living in a small home though. It is a whole movement that is meant to help you live in a better way, one that is friendlier to the environment. For example, many people who live in tiny homes choose to garden for their foods, perhaps wash dishes and take some baths in a nearby lake, and so on. It not only saves them money, but can help with keeping the environment healthy.

Getting started on this movement can be tough. There are so many things that you need to change. First, you have to get used to living in a smaller home. The average American home is over 2000 square feet. If you want to do the small home movement, you will need to go down by at least 1000 square feet while the tiny home would be at least 1600. That is quite a bit of space to get used to.

Each person who decides to go into the tiny home movement is going to have different mindsets about it. Some will start out with the idea that a small house is never a good idea. They may still want to chase the dream of having the biggest house on the block and can't consider how it would feel to be in such a tiny space all of the time.

Others may be really excited to finally get a chance to own their first home. They may be ready to just move into a place that isn't owned by someone else and would rather have the chance to sit back and relax in a home that is all their own. The tiny home movement is able to make this possible so much better than any housing market elsewhere and this makes it a more attainable, and attractive option for many people.

Some people may be looking at the tiny home movement and not quite ready to jump all in. They see all the benefits that are available with this kind of living, but are worried that the space will just be too restrictive or they just have too many people in their home to fit into the confines of a true tiny home. These people may be considering moving into a small home first, getting used to the ideas, and then making the switch later on.

And then there are the people who are all ready to just jump right into the experience. They are tired of living in a house that is too expensive, or they would like the chance to be much nicer to the environment. They love the idea of tiny home living and can't wait to get started. They will go all out and have all the little tips and tricks that are needed to make this home amazing for such a small space.

There are many different types of people when it comes to tiny home living. This kind of living is not going to be for everyone. It can be hard to live in such a small space, learning how to live with the bare minimum, and nothing else, that you truly need. But, for those who are ready for an adventure, who are tired of the way things currently are, and want a bit more freedom with their finances, this could be the right step to take!

It is all about a mindset. It can take some time, but eventually, you are going to learn why this is such a popular movement for a lot of people to enjoy!

The Benefits of Tiny Homes

The tiny home movement is one that has started to take off with a lot of steam. People like the idea of being able to live in a smaller area, but still own their own home and not have to worry about paying rent each month or having to save up for a big home that they may never be able to afford anyway. While living in a tiny home may not be the easiest thing to do all of the time, it does come with a ton of benefits that many people are finding are worth it all.

There are actually quite a few benefits that can come with moving into a tiny home. Many people may hear about this idea and assume that it is insane, that no one would want to give up so much in order to live in such a tiny place. Some may think it is silly or wonder how this kind of lifestyle is even going to work. But those who have researched up on the tiny home movement and who understand how this whole process works are ready to jump in and know that it just takes a bit of creativity to make it all come together.

If you are considering going into the tiny home movement, consider some of these benefits to make it a little easier

- Easier to afford—many people choose to go with a tiny home because it is much easier to afford. Depending on whether you make your own home or have someone else help you out, it could cost as low as a few hundred dollars. Share a plot of land with one or two other tiny homes, and you have a really affordable home that you can pay off in no time.
- Less mess—while those big houses may offer you some more space, they are also going to offer you a lot more when

it comes to messes. When you are in a small home, any mess is going to be big so you will need to keep things cleaned up all the time.

- Less materialistic—you will find that you become less materialistic when you live in a tiny home. You only have a limited amount of space so you will think hard before you decide to make another purchase that may not fit.
- Saves money—there are many ways that you can save money with tiny home living. First, the cost of the home will be lower. Next, you are less likely to buy things that you don't need and be careful with your purchases. In addition, you are going to find that your utility bill is much lower than before!
- Better for the environment—when you take away the waste and build something that is economical and just enough space for you to enjoy, you are helping to keep the environment healthy.

As you can see choosing to go with a tiny home can make all the difference when it comes to changing up your life. Consider looking into your very own tiny home and seeing how great it can be for your needs.

Chapter 2: Financing Your Tiny Home

One of the biggest appeals that many people like about the tiny home movement is the cost of getting started. You could easily pay more than $200,000 for a huge home that is on the market, but it is probably an older home, needs some work, and can be way over your budget already. Even if you build your own home, the costs are going to be high and it can take years for you to come up with the money for even a down payment.

This can make things difficult when you are first starting out. You want to have a place of your own, but everything is ridiculous. Luckily, financing and moving into a tiny home can be relatively easy. If you go through the process right, you may be able to get everything that you need without even needing to take out a loan.

Before you even get started on building your tiny home, or going through the process of finding a new tiny home to move into, you need to make sure that you get your financing in order. Some people are ready to go right away because they have been saving for many years to purchase a traditional home and instead decide to invest in a tiny home. Others may need to search for financing in other areas and this can sometimes take some time and effort. But knowing your options and getting started early can help make the process a bit smoother.

If you are interested in getting started on financing for your tiny home, consider these simple steps to help you do it the right way.

Ways to Finance the Tiny Home

Financing a tiny home can be relatively easy. If you are able to save for a few years, find a cheap plot of land that you can keep for your own or share with a few other people with the same ideas, and then build the house on your own, you can get the whole thing for a few thousand dollars. Of course, finding cheap land or having the ability to put together a whole house, even a tiny house, on your own, can be daunting for some people. Hiring a company to do the work for you may cost a bit more, but it is still really affordable.

No matter which direction you choose to go when it comes to building your home and getting ready to move in, check out these great ideas for financing that will make the whole thing easier.

Your Savings

If you have been considering purchasing your home, you probably already have a savings started up. Depending on how well you have done with the savings, you may already have enough to put down a sizeable down payment on the new tiny home. In some cases, you may be able to pay for it all outright. Think of how nice it would be to have a whole house paid for without having to worry about mortgage or anything else!

Even if you don't have enough to cover the whole cost of building a tiny home, any amount of savings can come in handy. It can help to reduce the amount that you owe on the home overall, makes it easier to find a mortgage company who will work with you, and can save you thousands of dollars over time.

Friends and Family

In some cases, you could consider asking friends and family to help you out. This is often a good source because your friends and family will be fine with just getting the same amount back, meaning no interest payments, and they are usually pretty easy to work with as long as you can find someone to help.

If you do go this route, make sure to draw up some agreement about how you will pay the money back and any terms that the two parties agree upon. This can help to keep the air clear between you and the other party and ensures that everyone is fine with the transaction.

Some people find that it is hard to ask friends and family outright for the money, or they don't know anyone who is able to give them that lump sum to help out. If this is the case for you, consider asking for it in smaller donations. For example, instead of receiving birthday or

Christmas gifs from those you love, ask them to put the money they would usually spend on gifts for you into a fund hat you will use for the new house. This keeps things easy and can even solve the Christmas shopping problem.

Manufacturer Financing

When you choose to go the route of having a company design and build your tiny home, you may be able to get some other sources of financing. There are many companies who make these kinds of homes who are also willing to give you a loan directly through them. They also have different payment options, are easier to work with than the banks, and can make your dreams of owning a tiny home much easier.

Bank Loans

Bank loans are probably the most traditional form of loan that you can get on your tiny home. Most people know to go to their bank if they are looking for a new loan and many banks have pretty favorable terms. But you do need to be aware that there are often a lot of rules that you need to follow in order to get the bank loan.

For example, when using a bank loan, you may need to put down a payment to get started, reach a certain credit score before getting the money, and the tiny home needs to meet all safety and building code procedures before you are given the money. You will be able to choose from two different types of loans, secured and unsecured. Unsecured are harder to get but they will allow you to get the money without putting anything up for collateral while the secured loan will need something to prove to the banks that you will pay it back, such as a boat or a car.

RV Loans

Sometimes you can use an RV loan in order to finance your tiny home. In fact, there are some tiny home manufacturers who label themselves as RV manufacturers so that you are better able to get this kind of loan. To get this loan on your tiny home, you will need to have an address somewhere else that you can consider a primary residence, good credit, and a steady income. The loan is for up to fifteen years and the interest rates are usually under 7 percent so you can get a pretty good deal if you shop around.

Peer to Peer Lending

This kind of lending has seen a lot of changes over the years. It is a great way to get some of the money that you need to finance the tiny home, as long as you can make an appealing case to others to lend you the money. You can put some of your information on the site, explaining that you want to build your tiny home, how much money you would need to complete this process, and even the repayment plans.

If someone is willing to help you out on those terms, you will both enter into an agreement that takes place and gives you the money. You will be responsible for paying back the money as promised and following all the rules like other loans do, but these are often a little easier to get, and sometimes with better terms, compared to bank loans.

Credit Cards

This is one option that you can use, but it is better to use up all the previous options first. Credit cards can make this kind of purchase, but the interest rate is really high and if you aren't able to pay it off within a few months, you are likely to pay thousands more on the tiny home than you would with a traditional loan. It is better to go with a different kind of loan or consider saving up rather than using your credit card.

Every person who decides to start living in a tiny home will have a different financing method that works the best for them. These are just a few suggestions that can get you going in the right direction to finding the money that you need to start this exciting new lifestyle.

Chapter 3: Location and Building Your Tiny Home

Once you have come up with the money that is needed to build your tiny home, it is time to find the location to place the tiny home and even to get building. Luckily, these steps do not have to be difficult as long as you are prepared to put in some work and you know exactly what you are getting into!

Finding the Perfect Location

Finding the perfect location can be different for everyone who goes into this process. Some people will just find a piece of land that is relatively cheap in their area. Others are looking to become a little more self-sufficient and so they will look around for a piece of land that is big enough and near enough natural resources that they can almost go off the grid. The location is often just up to your personal preferences.

If you are someone who wants to live off the land and really take he tiny home movement to another level, you should look out of town. There are many locations that are near streams, rivers, and even the forest that are basically abandoned. In some cases, you could even get the land for free, or relatively cheap, although you should check it all out to be sure ahead of time. This can allow you to clean your clothes in the river, grow your own garden, and even go hunting to get more food.

Many people are not that interested to going all out and going off the grid when they start tiny home living. It is perfectly fine to pick out a small plot of land that is located in your town and use that for the tiny home. Since the home will not take up very much space, you can settle for a smaller lot and still have plenty of room.

To save even more money on your land prices, consider going in on one plot with another person. You might know someone who is also considering going into the tiny home movement, you can both find a larger plat and split the cost. You can have a friendly neighbor and still plenty of space to build the home and have a backyard.

Building Your Tiny Home

Building a tiny home can be a great experience. You can get your hands nice and dirty and build a house that is your very own. If you are handy at building things or want to learn how to do all of this, building the tiny home can save you a lot of money. You still need to keep up with all the building codes, especially if you get a bank loan, so this can be a little bit scary for some who are just starting out.

Even if you don't know all of the building codes when you first get started. You can still do a great job. Many people who decide to do these homes on their own will speak with a contractor, or have them working along. This can still save a lot of money by allowing you to do most of the work, but you are bringing in a professional who will be able to make sure the house is safe.

When you are ready to get started, you will need to come up with a plan. You can design your own or you can choose to go through several that are available online to help you make the decision. This is one place where you will need to bring in the contractor. To get the permits to do the building, the floor plan needs to be approved and signed off by a contractor. Whether you are making your own or using another one, or even having the contractor write one out for you, it is important to make a floor plan that will work for the long term.

Consider everything that you would like to have inside of your tiny home. You would be surprised at how much can fit into this tiny space, but you do need to be realistic. Is a fancy kitchen really important or are you more concerned with finding somewhere to just sit back and relax? How many people are you going to try and fit into each space? All of these are important considerations before building.

You must also pick out high quality materials. While keeping costs low can be a top priority, you also need to remember that you plan to live in this house and the type of materials that you choose for your home will really show. Go with the higher quality so that you can really enjoy your new home and be comfortable.

During the building process, make sure that you are all ready to go. You may want to bring in one or two other people to help you out. Even when building a tiny home, it can be a lot of work. Having help can make things so much easier.

Building a tiny home can be really hard and if you don't have the time or the expertise, you may want to consider hiring another company to give you a hand. You will find that there are quite a few tiny home manufacturers you can choose to go with. Some of these are involved in manufacturing regular homes and do the tiny homes on the side, and other specialize in the tiny homes.

Hiring another company is often the choice that people will go with. They may be busy with their own jobs or feel that it is just too time consuming to try and do it all on their own. You can find financing, advice, and get the perfect floor plan when you are ready to go with another company rather than trying to go it all on your own.

Whether you are planning on making the tiny home on your own or you would like to hire someone else to help you out with building the home, it can be a great experience that you are going to love!

Chapter 4: Easy Space Hacks to Make Tiny Home Living Easier

Once you move into your tiny home, you are going to realize how low on space you really are. But there are a lot of great things that you can do in order to reduce your waste and to ensure that you are getting as much use out of the space as possible. Here are some easy space hacks that you can try out when organizing the kitchen in your tiny home kitchen.

Kitchen Ideas

Multiple uses

The most important thing that you can do in order to see success in your tiny home kitchen is to find items that can work for more than one purpose at a time. If you are able to find a pot that can work to cook food and also as a strainer, this can give you two items for one. Kitchen items often have a lot of great options that can combine the two purposes as long as you look around and learn to use a little creativity.

Find ways to hang things up

Anywhere that you are able to hang things up, you should. There are many places where you will be able to hang up items in the kitchen. You can use the ceiling to hang up pots, the walls to hang up spoons and other cooking utensils, and so on. Even consider hanging things up on the inside of your cupboards so you can store more items while still keeping them hidden away from sight.

Use the ceiling rather than cupboards

Hanging something from the ceiling and having this to be in charge of your pots and pans rather than taking up a lot of valuable space in the cupboards. These pots and pans are known for taking up a ton of space, and when you only get one or two cupboards in the whole house, this can be a bad thing.

Hanging some things from the ceiling can save so much space. You will need to put things up high enough that you are not going to hit your head, but this still leaves some room for you to reach up a bit and be able to get everything that you need in just a few minutes. Make sure that the hanging rack is sturdy and will stay in place so you aren't picking up a mess later on.

Shelf organizers

Shelf organizers can give you two to three times the space in your drawers and cupboard space. You may have many items inside of your cupboards that are pretty small and don't take up that much space. If you add in some shelf organizers, you could add an extra shelf in the same area. Place smaller items in the same area and get all the extra room that you need.

This is also a good place for you to add in a lazy susan. This can do a great job at organizing the really small items that you need and keeping all of your spices and herbs in one place that is easy to keep track of. You can spin around the product and find everything without having to make a mess out of your whole cupboard.

Divide up the drawers

You can get more out of your drawers if you learn how to divide them up. It can also help make things easier to find when you're looking for. When you put little dividers into each of the drawers, you will be able to put the silverware with the bigger spoons or to have the pots and pans with your Tupperware products. Consider adding in any dividers that you can think of in order to make the most out of the space that you have.

Make a counter a table

Your tiny home may not have the room that is needed in order to fit in a full sized table. You could consider using a counter as your table. You may have to take some time to clean up after you are done cooking, but this can save a lot of room when you don't have to stuff a table inside. Find a way to fold up the chairs against the wall to save even more space and your kitchen, and the rest of the house, will have more room than ever before.

Your kitchen can easily become crowded when it comes to being in a tiny home. And when the kitchen is tiny, you are going to have to find ways to keep it organized and contain as many of the items that you need as possible. Use these simple tips and you will be able to get the most out of your great new kitchen.

Chapter 5: Living Room

When it comes to the living room, you and your family are sure to spend a lot of time enjoying life in this area of your tiny home. This is also a good area that you are able to use in order to really do some good storage and if done properly, ensure that you are still getting a lot of functionality out of everything that you are doing. Here are some easy tips that you can use to make sure that you are getting the most out of your tiny home living room to add function and style to your area.

Use the walls

It doesn't matter what part of the home you are working on, you need to make the most out of the space that you have available. In any home, there is always a lot of space that is available on the walls. This is space that is just sitting there, and as long as you get some good hanging items and use it wisely, you can store a lot of the items that you plan to use in the home and keep it out of the way but still handy whenever needed.

There are a lot of cool items that you are able to use that help you to use the wall space well. You can use hanging items that let you drape items on top. You can pick to use some kinds of shelves that look nice but can easily be kept out of the way. Look at etsy and other sites to get some more ideas to make the home look amazing without having to give up on the style.

Have a multipurpose table

Your table can have so many purposes. In addition to being able to help you to hold cups and other items when you are sitting back and enjoying life in your tiny home, you can get a table that is able to store more items. You can choose to put blankets, cups, or other household items inside and know that they are safe and out of the way while you are still keeping the beautiful look in your home.

Avoid the end tables

End tables are really just taking up space inside of your living room. They don't have much of a purpose here and can just take up room where you will be able to put other things. It is best to just get rid of these tables and put in another bookcase or other space saving option. If you do decide to get an end table, make sure that it has plenty of storage space so you aren't wasting the space.

Put storage under the couch

Your couch can have a lot of use when it comes to your living room. You should put it to good use and store some items underneath it. You can consider using some little lifters that go under the legs of the couch and allow it to be up an extra few inches. You will barely notice this when you're sitting down on the couch, but you will love how it can fit some narrow boxes of storage underneath the couch and not having to find other storage areas.

Have furniture that can store

You do not have to choose the traditional furniture that you enjoyed when you were in your old home. While this stuff may have looked really nice in your old home, you do have some more options and need to make some changes. Take some time to look around and check out any furniture that you can find that has some storage inside. You could find couches that allow you to take off the cushions and hold blankets or other items. Think of how much room you could have in your home if you were able to host things right inside of the furniture you are sitting on.

Use the bookcases

Bookcases are a big lifesaver. You can put pretty much anything inside of a bookcase to put it out of the way, including extra food, books, and other items. You should consider having a few bookcases through your tiny home. This will keep things out of the way and save room on the floor. You can even consider adding in some doors to the bookcases so that you can hide any messes that come up and keep the house clean.

Hide-a-bed couches

If you are trying to fit multiple people in one area, or you don't have room for all the bedrooms that you need for everyone, a hide-a-bed couch can make a big difference. You can have guests sleep here or safe room on one or two of the rooms in your home. Just pull out the bed when it is needed and then you are ready to go whenever. The next day, fold the bed back in and you get all your room back.

Chapter 6: Bathroom

The bathroom can sometimes be the hardest room in the whole house to organize. There are a lot of items that you typically keep in the bathroom, but you may not have as much space as you would like when it comes to the tiny home. Here are some of the best tips that you can follow when you are ready to take care of that tiny home bathroom.

Back of the doors

The back of your doors in any room will free up so much space throughout the whole house. Think of it; the space behind your doors is one that you are most likely not using in the first place and ignoring it means that you are not using all of your space wisely in a tiny home. So take a look at the back of the door in your tiny bathroom and decide how it can be used for your advantage.

There are so many things that you are going to be able to fit on the back of your bathroom door. You can hang up the towels in this area, consider getting a show rack and hanging up other items that you need to get ready in the morning, and even find a way to hang up some clothes there so they are out of the way and ready for the morning. The possibilities are endless and you may be surprised at how much room you are freeing up.

Use travel size

You do not have to rely on the big sized bottles of bathroom supplies when you are organizing your bathroom. In fact, these can take up a ton of space and makes it difficult to fit anything else into the space. Travel sized shampoos, conditioners, and the like can make all the difference when it comes to space inside of the bathroom.

Hang towels on the wall

When it comes to the bathroom in your tiny home, you are probably going to have to give up on some of the luxuries that you enjoyed before. One of these luxuries is going to be having clean towels each day. You will most likely need to reduce the amount of towels that are in your home in the first place since these take up a lot of space and many families in these homes choose to go down to just one towel for each person.

You also have to be careful that you aren't taking up space in your cupboards by putting all of your towels inside. Hanging the towels up can help to save some room and still have them right where they are needed when you get cleaned up. You can hook the towels on the back of the door or find another place that is clear inside the bathroom.

Use storage above the toilet

The area above your toilet is one of the most underutilized areas in your whole home. When it comes to your tiny home you need to start putting it to some good use. Consider getting a cupboard or a shelf that will fit well right above the toilet and will still provide you with some of the storage room that your bathroom really needs.

Sometimes you may just choose to insert a shelf there and be done with the work and other times it is better to just put a little insert right above the toilet to get the feel. You must also choose between an open shelf and one that is just like your cupboards and can have the doors shut. No matter which option you choose, you are going to love how much extra space this gives you in the bathroom.

Bathroom caddy on the showerhead

You do not need to fit all of your bath time essentials into a cupboard when it comes to a small bathroom. Instead, consider getting a small caddy that you can use to keep it all out of place and ready to go. There are a few different options that you can give a try and they will each be ale to keep all that bathroom stuff right where you need it rather than in the way.

One option is to use a caddy that can hook on to the showerhead. This doesn't take up any shower space and as long as the showerhead is strong enough to be able to hold this, you should be fine. Make sure that it is small enough to fit into the shower but big enough to hold all your shampoo, conditioner, soap, and other items that you need in order to enjoy bath time.

Another option is to get a caddy that can hook to the wall. These would have some suction cups in place so you are able to just hook it anywhere, whether it fits the best inside of the shower or somewhere else. You can also move these caddies easily so if you need to get it out of your way, it won't be that big of a deal.

Add some cupboard space

Your bathroom is probably going to be a little bit on the small size in a tiny home. Most people simply have a toilet with a little sink, though you may have a shower if you make the area a little bit bigger. You should utilize as much area as possible for shelving to hold all the items that you would like to put inside of the tiny bathroom. This makes it easier to keep things out of the way and to have a nice looking bathroom even when you are short on space.

Shower over the toilet

You are going to have to be really smart when it comes to the amount of space that you have in your bathroom. Some people have found that making a contraption that allows the shower to be over the shower, or over the sink, can help to save space and be really efficient. You can talk to your contractor about how to get this all set up for the best results!

Outside shower

Many times you will choose to put most of your available space in the tiny home to some of the other rooms and your bathroom is going to end up pretty small. This may mean that you will not have room for a ton of shower space. One solution to this is to have a shower that is available outside. While you may need to be a bit careful about doing this if you have neighbors, it can save a lot of space and still allow you a chance to enjoy a good shower when you're ready to get clean.

Boxes are your friend

You should consider using boxes to help keep things organized inside of your bathroom. There are a lot of items that you are going to need to keep track of when you're dealing with the bathroom, and boxes could be the thing that you need to use to keep everything together and to avoid wasting so much time on trying to find things when you need them.

You should pick out a few boxes, in any color, that you like and which will still fit well into the space that you have in your tiny home. You will then need to go through all of your bathroom items and sort them in any way that you choose. Perhaps bath stuff can be in one pile while cleaning supplies, makeup, and so on can be in another. This will make it so much easier to find the items when you need them and can avoid some of the issues that come with clutter.

Keeping the bathroom organized and ready to go can be one of the hardest parts. There seems to be a lot of items that we like to keep in our bathrooms and these items can quickly get messed up and go all over the place. Learning how to keep everything in order and to use the most out of your space in the bathroom can make a big difference in how well it looks overall.

Chapter 7: Bedrooms

Your bedroom is one of those areas that can fill up quickly. A lot of random items like to find their way inside of the bedroom, and if you aren't careful with using the space wisely and finding ways to be as organized as possible, you are going to end up in trouble pretty quickly. But, if you choose to follow some of the tips that are in this section, you can have an amazing bedroom with lots of space when you are living in your tiny home.

Lift up the bed

Your bed is a great place to store some of the items that are just in your way or that you need to save for another season. If your bed is tall enough, you may be able to just slip some things underneath. But you can also consider getting a few risers to put under the feet of your bed and lifting it up even a few inches more. You are not going to notice that much of a shift in the bed, but this could be the key to adding a few more boxes under the bed.

Along with this idea, consider getting a few plastic boxes. Long and thin are the best option. You can then choose to use this as a kind of dresser or make this your storage unit to hold the winter coats and snow pants and bringing them out as soon as the weather changes. Your uses for this space can be different than someone else's, but as long as it saves you some room in the tiny home, you are doing a good job.

Use the back of the door

The back of the door can be your greatest asset when it comes to living in a tiny home. This is space that you aren't really using, so put it to some good use. You can find some cute little hangers to put on the door and store everything there. Lots of people like to put some show holders on the back so they can put some random objects up and out of the way. There are many options that will just hang over the top of the door and they won't really take up all that much space. But the amount of space these items can save you when you clear out the clutter is amazing.

Use double hangers

When picking out your hangers, choose the ones that allow you to hang a few clothes on the same hanger. Once it is full, this kind of hanger will allow you to bring it down to the ground, keeping all the clothes together and off the floor, but having you use more vertical space rather than all the horizontal. Depending on the size of hanger that you choose, you could fit ten or more outfits in the same amount of space where you used to hang one or two items. Think of all the space that you are going to be able to save with this one great invention in your tiny closet.

Jewelry hanger

A jewelry box may seem like a good idea, but your jewelry can easily get all tangled up and become a mess. Plus, you may not have the room for a dresser or other item to hold the jewelry box and then where are you going to hang all of this stuff?

Instead of relying on a jewelry box, it is time to get creative and see what you are able to do with some ideas on the wall. Make your own jewelry hanger that can go on any free space in your room and will help to keep the jewelry from getting stuck together and makes the room look nice as well. Experiment with a few different options to find the one that is the best for your personal tastes and enjoy how easy it is to grab the piece of jewelry that you want without all the untangling hassle.

Bed storage

You have a lot of choices when it comes to picking out the new bed that is in your home. One thing that you can choose is the storage that comes with the bed. Some people have opted to put little drawers in the base of their beds. These can then hold their clothes and other items in one secure location and can work as the dresser, rather than trying to find room for this piece of furniture, in the tiny home.

Another option that is available is to store things under the mattress. There are beds that you can lift up the mattress a bit and have a whole storage unit underneath. Store some of your pillows and blankets as well as anything else that you need in there and it is always going to be out of your way.

Vacuum Sealed Storage

If you have some items that you need to store for the winter, consider getting some of those vacuum sealed storage containers. These are like big bags that you can stick coats, jackets, blankets, and more inside. Then you just vacuum out the air and are left with a relatively thin package holding all these items rather than each one taking up a lot of space. Have a few of these on hand and use them each time you switch out of the seasons. This can make more room in your home but ensures that you have everything you need as the seasons change.

Fold-away beds

There are many new inventions when it comes to the bed that you can choose to use. No longer are you stuck with one of the traditional options in beds and instead you can choose to go with something that is a bit different. Some people like the idea of a fold-away bed. These are popular because they can provide a full sized bed in the evening, but when morning arrives, you simply need to fold up the bed and it is ready to leave open some much needed space in the room.

You can even choose to go with an air mattress. These are really inexpensive and can be put up and taken down in just a few minutes. You can then fold up the air mattress in the morning and put it somewhere that is completely out of the way, but at night while you are sleeping, it can be comfortable and big enough to fit what is needed.

Taking care of the space that is inside of your tiny home is going to be a challenge. You need to be able to think ahead and figure out what you actually need inside of the tiny home and what is going to just cause big headaches when you try to fit it in. Using some of these great tips in your bedroom can save the time and headache that you have so that you can get into that home and be comfortable.

Chapter 8: Tips and Tricks to Understand Tiny Home Living

Getting started on the tiny home movement can be a life changing event. You want to be able to make some major changes to your life and find a home that is economical and environmentally friendly, but understanding what it is going to take to succeed can take some experience and time. When you are ready to get started on the tiny home movement, make sure to read through some of these tips to see the best results!

Realize how much space is available

One thing that a lot of people don't realize is just how small a tiny home can be. They are so used to seeing the huge houses that are always on the market, but it can be hard to imagine just how much space you are going to deal with once you move into the tiny home. 400 square feet or less is not really a lot of space and you need to be really organized and prepare to make this work.

If you are able to, consider asking a friend or family you know who already lives in a tiny home and take a look around the space. You can also go and visit a tiny home manufacturer and take a tour of one of their models. This can help you to see how much space you are actually going to have to work with and can help you with your whole planning.

Learn how to organize

Organization is going to become your best friend when you move into a tiny home. You are going to be really limited on the amount of space that you get to use in this new home, and even a few things on the floor or lying about can really take up some of the valuable space that you need and make a mess.

So before even moving into the tiny home, consider learning some organization skills. These can help you to keep all your items in the right location, saves you time, and makes the house look as clean as possible. Organization doesn't have to be a challenge, and you may even find that it is easier than before once you get rid of many of your possessions and move into the tiny home.

Don't go too crazy on the accessories

Accessories can make a house a home. There are many great wall hangings, picture frames, and so much more that you may want to add to the home, but these are just going to be a waste of space. You could use that space on the wall, the table, and everywhere else to store more items that you need to actually get through the day in this home.

If you just must have some accessories in your home, learn how to make them multi-functional. Do not purchase anything that is not able to work in multiple functions. You can get that nice wall hanging, but make sure that it can work well for helping to store some of your other personal items.

Use your wall space

There is nothing more valuable than your wall space when it comes to living in a tiny home. You are not going to have the benefit of having more space going horizontally, but your vertical space, the walls, will have plenty of space for you to use. Learn how to hang things up and store along the walls, and you will be able to get so much more into the home.

Figure out how to minimize

You are not going to be able to bring all of your material possessions along with you when moving into a tiny home. While it would be nice to bring every item that you own, you are going to be really limited on space. You need to learn how to bring just the items that you will need in order to make it through, and get rid of everything else.

You have to be really aware of all the things that you use during the day. You will not need to bring all of the kid toys, twenty towels, and every piece of clothing item that you have ever owned. You will need to go through each room and get it down to the bare minimum that you are able to deal with.

While going through your items, make sure to consider whether you are able to replace a few items for one that can do all the same work. There are many items that can be used for two or three different tasks. You can get rid of the three items and replace them with just one, finding that it is much easier to save space.

If you are still looking to get some of the money to get the tiny home financed, consider having a garage sale with these items. You are most likely getting rid of quite a few items, and you could easily have some savings money to help out.

Use the elements around you

Using the elements that are present all around you can make a big difference on how well you are going to do in the tiny home. Some people assume that they need to fit everything into their tiny home and can feel stressed out when it just doesn't work that well for them. But when you place the home in the right location and start to use the area that is around you, you will find that you have more room than you could imagine.

For example, consider placing your home near a local river or a lake. This is a natural water source that you will be able to use to your full advantage. You can take some of your baths in the lake or the river, saving room on the shower you choose. You can wash your dishes and clothes in the water, saving room on a washer and dryer.

Consider using the outside to grow some of your food as well. Growing a garden is a common practice for those who live in a tiny home. This allows you to grow some fresh produce and herbs without taking up space in your limited pantry. Consider starting out with just a few types of produce and slowly expanding as you get more used to the process.

Living in a tiny home can take some practice and patients to get all done. But when you work hard to make it happen, and realize that you will need to make some sacrifices, you will find that this is one of the best ways of living that you could imagine!

Conclusion

The tiny home movement is starting to take the world by storm. Many people are tired of how insane modern houses are becoming and how hard it can be to purchase your first home. Most of the time these homes are too big for the family who will use them, and this can cause a lot of waste. People are turning to the tiny home movement in order to get an affordable and environmentally friendly home.

This guidebook is going to take some time to explain more about the tiny home movement and some of the steps that you can take in order to see some success with living in such a tiny home. From a deeper understanding of what the tiny home movement is all about to some tips to make it easier, you are going to find all the answers that you need. Take a look through this guidebook and learn everything that you need in order to see some success with living in a tiny home.

Backyard Chickens
A Beginners Guide To Raising Backyard Chicken
Nancy Ross

Table of Contents

Introduction

Chapter 1: The Basics of Raising Chickens in Your Backyard

Chapter 2: Getting Setup to Bring the Chickens Home

Chapter 3: The Best Backyard Breeds

Chapter 4: Understanding the Basic Behaviors of Your Chicken

Chapter 5: Medical Issues With Your Chickens

Chapter 6: Making Money With Your Chickens

Conclusion

Introduction

One of the biggest trends that is going on for many families right now is the idea of self-sufficiency. Some families are tired of paying the high prices when they go to the grocery store each month while others are worried that there will be a huge food shortage due to government interference or a natural disaster sometimes in the near future and they want to be prepared. While there are several things that you can do to start out on this self-sufficiency lifestyle, raising chickens is probably one of the easiest, as well as most fun, methods that you can use to take care of everything.

This guidebook is going to help you learn how to get started with raising your own chickens from home. This can actually be a really affordable process; you simply need to either build your own coop or purchase one, find some good pellet food, and purchase the chickens. The upfront costs may be a bit higher, but considering the chickens don't eat much food, the coop can be reused, and you can hatch your own chickens so as to never have to purchase them again, this quickly becomes affordable.

These are just a few things that are going to be discussed in this guidebook. In addition to picking out the right breed of chicken for your needs and getting the coop set up, we are going to take some time to look at the different foods that you can feed your chicken, what is considered normal behavior in a chicken, how to avoid many common health and social problems with your chickens, how to make money from raising chickens in your backyard, and even how to really benefit from all this hard work by using the eggs and meat for food.

Raising chickens can be one of the most rewarding experiences in your life. They are really easy to take care of as long as you provide them with the right nutrition and a space to fall asleep at night, and you will not have to spend a lot of money on getting it all set up. But for all the joy and bonding experience that you will be able to share with your children over raising the chickens and the great high quality eggs and meat that can now be put on your table, this is definitely a process that you should consider. Use this guidebook to learn everything that you need to know in order to get started on the right path to beginning your own chicken farm in your backyard.

Chapter 1: The Basics of Raising Chickens in Your Backyard

Have you ever dreamed about being self-sufficient and being able to take care of your own needs from your own backyard? Do you like the idea of fresh eggs in the morning, being in control of some of your own food supply, or even to have a chance to work on 4H projects and other big events? Backyard farming may be the answer that you need to make all of this and more occur without having to leave your home.

Raising chickens in your backyard can be an affordable way to help take care of your family. While chicken and eggs can be really expensive at the traditional grocery store, they can be really affordable to raise in the back. And with a simple coop and some attention, the chickens can often thrive and provide you with everything that you need. Add on a nice learning experience for the kids, and you are going to have everything that you need for a good family bonding experience.

Benefits of Backyard Chickens

You may be surprised at the amount of benefits that you can enjoy when you choose to do backyard chicken raising. First, chickens are kind of funny to watch as they grow up. There are many varieties that you have to choose from, as well as colors and shapes, and many of them have some quirky behaviors. This could be the way to get your family away from the computer and television screens and to get outside.

Taking care of chickens can be pretty simple. You need to make them a safe home to live in, make sure that they don't get sick, and give them the proper food. In many cases, the chickens are going to be able to eat their own foods such as pests, grasshoppers, and ticks so you can clear out some of these issues in the backyard and don't have to obsess about how much food you are feeding them.

Many families choose to raise chickens in order to get all of the great fresh eggs right away. These eggs are amazing, with no more pale yolks or water whites and everything is more likely to be perfect with as much nutrition as you can pack into the eggs. These eggs are lower in cholesterol as well as higher in many vitamins and the omega-3 fatty acids to help you keep healthier.

But one of the best reasons to choose to go with backyard chickens is because of the family bond that they can include into your family. The family will need to work together to get the chickens all set up and to help feed them. Children can learn a lot about responsibility when you let them help with raising the chickens. It can be time spent together and outside rather than sitting in front of a screen all day!

There are so many reasons to choose to raise chickens in your backyard. They give you a lot of benefits and considering raising chickens doesn't take too much of your time or energy, they are the perfect addition to your own backyard, even when you are short on space.

What You Need to Get Started

Getting started with your backyard chickens is a pretty simple process. You will need to follow just a few steps and you can start raising those chickens in no time. The first thing that you will need to do is decide on the breed of chicken that you would like to have. There are many different options and some are going to do better in certain areas while others may not. You will also need to be careful with the temperament of the different birds and the level of care so take some time to look through the different options.

You will then need to pick out a place for your chickens to grow up. It needs to have some room for the amount of chickens that you would like to keep in your backyard, room for the coop, and even some room for the chickens to move around and be free range. You also probably want a little bit more room for you to be able to walk around the backyard so be reasonable with the amount of space that is available and how many chickens you will be able to keep in one place.

Now it is time to get everything set up. You will need to get the coop all set up. You may choose to build your own coop, which allows you to specialize it to your space and tastes a bit more, or you can choose to go with one that is already made to save a bit of time. Make sure that it is going to have enough room for the amount of chickens that you are going to need and will be pretty sturdy.

Picking out the right kind of food for your backyard chickens is important as well. It is a good idea to keep around some high quality chicken feed to make things easier and help your chickens to get all the nutrition that they need. But keep in mind that the chickens are going to enjoy the pests in your backyard as a nice treat so you won't have to worry as much about feeding a ton of food.

Grooming, taking time to make a comfortable place for the chickens, and even taking care of their medical needs can all be important parts of the whole chicken raising process. You will need to learn what your chickens will need to ensure that they stay healthy and are getting all the care that they need.

Compared to the amount of benefits that you can get out of the chickens and the relatively low amount of work that you will need to do with them, chickens can often be one of the best animals to add into your personal life.

Chapter 2: Getting Setup to Bring the Chickens Home

You may need to do a little bit of preparation before bringing the chickens home. You will want to make sure that they have the right shelter, as well as the right kind of food, to be comfortable and ready to lay all of those eggs. Make sure to follow some of these suggestions to ensure that your chickens are being taken care of properly and you are getting the most out of all this hard work.

Getting the Coop Set Up

Before you bring home your new chickens, you need to make sure that they have a place to call home. There are many different ideas that you can use to make your own chicken coop, or you can purchase one at the store to ensure it is nice and sturdy, but you need to find the ideas that will fit the best in your own backyard, will hold the amount of chickens that you need, and which will not be too big of a hassle to handle.

Many people choose to just purchase a chicken coop. This allows them to talk to someone who can help them out some more and makes it easier to get the right size and shape for their needs. If you are choosing to build your own coop, which can be a great experience to really get out there and be involved and saves you some money, consider looking at the different floor plans that work in your backyard and for your chickens.

Some of the things that you should keep in mind when it comes to creating your own chicken coop or deciding where you should place it include:

- Find some shade—you do not want to place the chicken coop somewhere that is in direct sunlight all day long. Find some shade so the chickens can get a break. This also gives them a little protection if the winter or fall elements start to get harsh.
- Elevate the nesting floor—if you put this up a few feet, it can help to keep the chicken's feet dry when the weather gets wet. You can add in a ramp so the chickens are able to get easily up and down.
- Add in some lights—the inside of the chicken coop can get dark, especially at night. Add in some lights to help make it easier to see inside and to even help the chickens to get more sun to lay more eggs.
- Feather the nest—your coop is not going to be done until you add in some roosting perches and nesting boxes. You can add in some wicker baskets with straw or add in a bit of feathers to help make the nest as comfortable as possible.
- Choose hardware carefully—make sure that you find the hardware that is resistant to predators and will keep the

chickens safe. Metal latches that are secure and can't be opened with a paw can keep the chickens safe.

- Don't forget the outdoor space—your chickens are not going to want to spend all their time inside the chicken coop. Create an outdoor space that allows them to move around a lot and keeps them safe. For your backyard you could use the back fence or create an area of your own.
- Add in the vents—the chickens can start to feel sick if the air isn't circulating within the coop. Add in some screened gaps between the walls so that the hot air can get out without causing some drafts.
- Think about convenience—not only should the chicken coop be comfortable for the chickens, you need to make it easy for regular cleaning, to walk around, and for gathering the eggs. Think this through when figuring out the right setting for your needs.
- Recycling can be your friend—sometimes, using old things that are around the home can help out with the chicken coop. Your old trash will work great to create a safe and secure place for the chickens.
- Think about how much room the chickens need—the smaller coop may be a bit cheaper, but if you have twenty chickens, it may be time to think about something bigger. Each chicken is going to need at least a few feet each to be comfortable and move around so consider this when building or purchasing the chicken coop.

When you put everything together, you need to have a chicken coop that is convenient for the chickens, allows for enough space for the chickens to move around and be comfortable, and that is easy to clean out and to gather the eggs that you need. There are many different options that you can choose from with this, but you need to find the one that works the best for your needs and in your area.

Picking Out the Right Foods

One question that a lot of people have when they first bring home their chickens is what they should feed the animals. They want to make sure that the chickens are going to stay healthy and happy, but what types of foods are going to help out with this process. You will want to feed your chickens a balanced and complete diet so that they are able to lay better eggs and even to stay healthy. Chickens like to eat a wide variety of foods in order to help them get all their nutrition, so offering up some variety can make the difference.

The first thing that you should offer is a good quality pellet for poultry. There are dispensers that help out a lot in keeping the pellets dry, even if you leave them outside for a bit, so your chickens are willing to eat them up and get the nutrition. You can also try some grains, such as corn and wheat to help add in a bit more nutrition to the meals.

Fresh food can be great for your chickens to add in some more nutrition. Fresh fruits and vegetables can do really well for the chickens and you can add them into the diet each day and options like spinach, silverbeet, cabbage, and various fruit and vegetable peels can really add in the nutrition.

In some cases you can add in a bit of table food to your chicken's diet. You can include legumes, bread, beans, cooked pasta, rolled oats, and wholemeal rice. You should always talk to your veterinarian to ensure that you aren't giving something that is going to cause some harm to the body of your chicken.

For those chickens who are going to be laying quite a few eggs for you, try to add in a high calcium supplement. A good way to do this is to take an egg shell and ground it into a powder before adding it into the regular feed. Many pellets are layered with some calcium as well so that the chickens are able to stay healthy and you will keep getting all those delicious eggs that you are looking for.

And of course, your chickens are going to love eating at some of the pests that you have in your backyard. These are a special treat to the chickens so adding them in on occasion can be fun. You can choose to allow the chickens to

Chapter 3: The Best Backyard Breeds

Now that everything is all set up, it is time to pick out the breed that you would like to bring home. There are many breeds of chickens, but not all of them are going to work the best in your backyard. Some just don't do well for producing eggs while others may not do the best in colder climates because of the heat. You will need to choose carefully to decide which chickens are going to be the right one for your family.

The first thing that you should consider when picking out a chicken is the temperament. You want a breed that is easy to get along with and won't mind being touched or followed, especially if you have some younger children. Chickens are that are a bit more vocal and loud may have trouble being around smaller children and should be avoided.

You will also need to consider how many eggs the chicken is able to produce. If you would like to have a good egg laying chicken, you need to pick a breed that will produce at least a few eggs each week. This is a challenge when first getting started and you don't want to put in all that hard work to find out you're wrong.

The weather in your area is going to make a big difference. Some chickens do poorly in cooler temperatures so if you live up in the north, you should not choose those breeds. On the other hand, there are several types of chickens that can do pretty well in the winter due to their thick coats and these may be the ones that you should go with.

Ultimately, it comes down to your personal preferences. There are many differences and similarities that come with each of the chicken types and you need to find the one that you like the best, whether it is because of the color of the bird, if they do well with children, or how well the chicken does in the cold.

The Plymouth Rock

The first kind of backyard chicken that you should consider is the Plymouth Rock. This breed has a lot of different varieties with the most popular options being the barred and the white. It is really friendly, making it perfect for hanging around in the backyard and with younger kids. It is good for those who are just starting out with the backyard chickens and need something that is sturdy and doesn't need a lot of care.

This bird is able to reach a big weight of almost 9.5 pounds, which means they are going to be good for eating the meat. They are also perfect for laying brown eggs on a consistent basis. If you would like to have a chicken that can produce a lot of brown eggs each day and who will be good as a meat bird when it comes time to prepare for Thanksgiving, the Plymouth Rock chicken is the right option.

The Rhode Island Red

You can recognize this kind of bird by the rust colored feathers that are easy to spot from a mile away and it is one of first birds that hobbyists will choose when it comes to their backyard chickens. They are not going to get as big as the Plymouth Rock variety, but they are still a pretty big bird and they do well with hatching a lot of eggs so it is a good option for most families to choose.

The Leghorn

You might want to make sure that you have some experience under your belt before choosing to go with the Leghorn. These are a little bit noisier and flighty compared to the other breeds and they may not like that little children are messing with them or all the loud noise that can come from this. But if you would like to get a chicken that is really good for the eggs, the Leghorn is one of the best for this due to their special breeding.

The Jersey Giant

This is the bird that you are going to choose if you really want a bird that is good for getting the meat from. This one is from America and if you feed them well and keep them happy, you will find that the Jersey Giant is able to get to a weight of 13 pounds in no time. This is one of the most popular breeds to choose if you would like to get a chicken that is mainly for the meat. There are a few different varieties that you are able to choose from and they all reach about the same size so you will be able to get a nice big bird.

Ameracaunas

To find this bird, you need to look for the chicken that has the fluffy feathers all around its head. These are one of the best known for raising blue colored eggs and they are really good for pets. For a family farm, they will work well with kids and the children may like to see the eggs of different colors as well as all the feathers that are on the chickens' head.

While this kind of chicken does a great job at helping to lay a lot of eggs and can be perfect if this is the main purpose that you want out of this bird, they are not good for slaughtering. These birds do not reach really big weights and the meat is going to be minimal when eating. If you want some eggs from the bird, this is the breed to go with but if you are looking for more of a meat giver, you should pick another option.

Orpington

For the person who is brand new to the idea of chicken farming in their backyard, this is a great breed to start with. They are great for laying a larger amount of brown eggs and their personality is great for just placing in the backyard and taking care of on occasion, and they do well with younger children. In fact, the Orpington likes to have contact from humans and can even jump on humans as you try to feed them so they won't have any issues with the children playing with the chicks. In fact, even the adult birds like to get attention and will sit calmly in a lap before going to sleep.

The Orpington is not only good for laying some of the best eggs. You will find that they are a bigger bird, often getting to more than eight pounds so they can make for some good eating. They are a really hardy chicken and can tolerate the colder weather pretty well so they are perfect for being in the northern climates.

Cornish

Next on the list is the Cornish chicken. This chicken is really popular for those who want to raise chickens for meat because this chicken is able to grow really fast. If you have a male Cornish chicken, you can expect them to get around 11 pounds and the hen can get to 8 pounds or more. And since they have some white plumage, you are not going to need to worry about having a pigment in the skin.

This breed is not really as active as some of the other breeds of chicken, so it is easier to keep them in one area and you will not have to waste a lot of time chasing them around and keeping them in their coop. They are also really good at living through the colder weather climates. But since these birds are slower and aren't really good at defending themselves, this is not a good choice if you are going to have a mixed flock.

Silkie

This breed is considered an ornamental breed. If you are looking to keep the chickens as a pet at the home, the Silkie is one of the best choices. They are really tame compared to some of the other breeds and they are pretty small so you will not have to chase them around to keep them contained. In addition, the hens are really good as mothers so you can hatch the fertile eggs and not have to do as much work. Even if the original mother is lost, the hens will become foster mothers and take care of any new babies that you add into the flock.

Silkies have some really great features. Their face is going to look similar to the Shiatsu dog and they have five toes, most chickens only have four toes, and black skin. They do well when they are kept in close confinement, but if you are having more than one type of chicken in the area, make sure to keep them separated from the flock. You should also take care during colder weather because their crest feathers will freeze in the cold.

These are just a few of the options that you can choose when it comes to picking out a chicken that you will like. You will need to pick whether you would like a chicken that is good at laying eggs or one that is better as a meat provider, or even one that can do the combination of the two. Once you find the chicken, or combination of chickens, that work the best for you, the rest of the process can be so much easier!

Chapter 4: Understanding the Basic Behaviors of Your Chicken

Once you bring home a chicken, you may be confused about how they should behave. Unless you have been raised on a farm or around other animals most of your life, it can be confusing to know whether a certain behavior is normal or not. In this chapter, we will take some time to explore the normal behaviors of your new pets and what you should concentrate on for raising them right.

Watching your flock of chickens can be really entertaining. Most of the time you will notice that chickens have a lot of complex interactions with other chickens and a lot of interesting behaviors. Just like other domesticated animals, you will notice that chickens are the happiest when they are able to stay in a group, especially a group of their own kind.

Without knowing more about these behaviors, you are going to have a hard time figuring out how to raise them properly. While raising chickens can be a great hobby to try out, whether you choose to raise them for egg production, meat, or just as pets, it is important for you to learn how to recognize certain behaviors and take good care of your chickens.

Sleeping Chickens

First off, we will look at how chickens act when they are sleeping. You will notice that when your chickens go to sleep, they will really fall asleep. Simply by making an area completely dark, your chickens are going to fall into a stupor. This is why they become such an easy target for predators because once it gets dark, they are not going to try and escape from anything or defend themselves.

Since the chickens are vulnerable to this issue when they are sleeping, they are going to roost off the ground during sleeping. This is why most coops are going to have a roost that is up a few feet to make the chickens feel a little more comfortable. Chickens also like to fall asleep in the same spot so you will notice that once the chickens recognize the coop as their new home, they will automatically go back there if they've escaped during the day or if you allow them to roam.

One tip to remember is that when catching your chickens, wait until it is dark. During the day the chicken may be more willing to wander around and can be a little bit hard to catch. But at night, the chickens are going to fall into that stupor and go to sleep. This means they aren't going to run around and if you go out a bit after dark with some flashlights, you will be able to catch them without issues.

Socializing Behaviors of Chickens

When it comes to your chicken, it is going to be all about the family. This means that you do not want to purchase just one chicken unless you are fine with the chicken making you a part of the family. Most chickens are happiest when they are in a flock and are able to socialize with other similar chickens.

This being said, chickens do have some special rules that they follow when it comes to forming their own flocks or family. In the wild, chickens are going to form into small flocks, usually with no more than 15 birds being in the very largest of flocks. Out of each of these flocks in the wild, there will only be one rooster.

The ranking system in the flock is going to begin right when the chick hatches, or when the chickens are put together in your backyard. The hens will follow their own kind of ranking system that is different from the roosters and it will not be long before each member of this group knows where it belongs. Of course, there may be some times when squabbling or battles will occur during this time. The best way to keep these to a minimum is to just have one rooster in place and there are fifteen or fewer chickens all together.

Order is really important when it comes to the flock. For example, the dominant hen is the one who gets to eat first, is the first one to pick where she would like to lay her eggs or roost, and can take away food from the lower ranked hens. And then they go down in the ranking from there. If the flocks have enough space and are small enough, the hens will usually avoid issues with fighting and will simply pick the order and go about their daily life.

Roosters are also going to establish a kind of ranking system, especially if there is two or more in the same flock. If you place a group of roosters together without having hens in place will just start to fight. But if it is a regular flock compromised of mainly hens but still more than one rooster, there will be a kind of uneasy truce to make a ranking. Often this will turn into more intense fighting later on and one or both of the roosters may die, which is why it is best to keep them separated.

If you have a larger backyard and are able to allow the chickens to move around freely, you may be able to have more than one rooster around because each one is going to be able to create their own flock without the fights. In these cases, each rooster will ignore the others, except for maybe a few spats. Of course, there are many different types of breeds and some are going to be a bit more aggressive than others. Keep in mind that if a rooster starts to become aggressive towards you, it is best to just use them for meat rather than fighting with that hassle.

The rooster is always going to be the leader against the hens. The rooster will be allowed to get whatever he wants and right when he wants it. Often the rooster is not going to want the hens to squabble a lot so this can help to reduce the amount of fighting that you have between the hens. But, the rooster will usually allow all the hens to eat along with him, as long as no one tries to pull ranks. In some intense fights between the other hens, the rooster may step in to help resolve the problem.

The rooster does not have to be the oldest or biggest in the flock. As long as the flock ends up being mature, he is going to become the leader of the coop. The rooster is not just about ruling over the hens though; he is also going to be their guide, protector, and basically lover. He will stand the guard over the hens when they eat, show them where to get the best things to eat, and will even show them to where the best places to nest are. He is their protector and as such, he is usually given some respect in the coop.

In most flocks, the roosters are going to have a favorite hen. This usually turns out to be the dominant hen in the flock, but not always, and they are good at treating their ladies well. The rooster is going to mate more with the one who is their favorite, but he will not ignore any of the hens and give them attention from time to time.

The Romance of Hens and Roosters

If you are looking to get some good eggs from your hens, you will need to have the rooster mate with these hens. Roosters do not have a big courtship ritual when compared to other types of birds, and the amount and type or romancing will vary depending on the type of rooster.

When the rooster is ready to mate with a hen, he will create his own tiptoelike walk. He will get in this stance and approach the hen, usually strutting around her a few times after he goes by. When the hen is approached in this way, they will crouch down before moving their tail to the one side to show they are in agreement.

The rooster is able to mate a few times a day. Younger roosters may try to mate a few times one right after the other, but in most cases, he will try to spread this throughout the day. When the mating process is done, the chickens are going to preen their feathers and then move on with their day. A rooster is even able to mate with a hen even if he is infertile, meaning that older roosters as well as those in the cold could still be mating.

Hens Without Roosters

Hens are not going to be lost if you don't have a rooster in the coop. In fact, they are able to even lay eggs on their own. The hen is going to be born with all of the eggs that her body will ever have, and the hen will lay all of these eggs for the rest of her life, or until there are no more eggs, whether or not the rooster is around.

The amount of eggs that the hen will lay varies depending on each individual as well as the type of bread. For the most part, the hen is going to lay their biggest amount of eggs within the first three years and after this time you should not expect to get very much out of them.

When the hen lays an egg without a rooster being around, the eggs will be infertile. These are the eggs that you will eat for breakfast because there are no baby chickens inside. The hormonal cycle of the chicken will have the eggs come out whether the rooster comes out. If you are just interested in having some good eggs to enjoy for breakfast, you can just pick out some hens and not bring home a rooster. On the other hand, if you would like the chance to raise baby chicks from home, a rooster can help to fertilize the eggs for this to happen.

Chicken Bath Time

Another issue to explore is bath time for the chickens. They aren't that fond of getting wet, but they do like to take some time kicking around and playing in the mud. Any time that some loose soil gets into the coop, you will find that the chickens are trying to take a bath in it, which can make them really messy.

Chickens are known for scratching out a depression in the soil, usually big enough to fit their whole body inside, and then lie down right in this depression. With the dirt that they took out of the hole, the chickens will throw right onto their feathers and shake it around. This seems to make the chicken very happy and it also is a good way to keep some of the parasites away.

While it may be a little bit annoying that the chickens are digging big depressions into your backyard, there isn't much of a way to stop this. You could put up a fence to contain them to one area instead of letting them do this digging all throughout the yard, or even give them a big box of sand to use for this process. But you will not be able to stop the chickens from going through this process.

As you can see, taking care of chickens doesn't take a lot of work. Just learning about some of their social behaviors and how they like to behave can make a big difference when it comes to how well you are going to be able to take care of them. Learn these behaviors and give the chickens the care that they need, and you are sure to have the perfect flock in your backyard.

Chapter 5: Medical Issues With Your Chickens

Common Health Concerns for Chickens

For the most part, raising your chickens will be simple. You will need to provide them with some friends to hang out with, keep the coop clean, and make sure that they get plenty of good food to help them grow healthy. But there are times when they are going to need some special care and attention because they are not behaving in a normal way or they are sick. Here are some of the most common health concerns that can occur with your chickens and how you can take care of each issue.

Picking

There are going to be ties when the chicken is going to peck at another's feathers and the skin. This is a process that is called picking and it is actually pretty normal for chickens, but you should watch out for it. In some severe instances, the chicken is going to be able to draw blood from this interaction and once the blood comes out, the problem is going to escalate. Chickens are attracted to blood and to the color red and picking can even lead to death.

Most of the time picking is going to occur when there are issues that are annoying the chickens. You may notice this issue if the chickens are not getting enough water or food, the light is too bright or left on for too long, or you just have a problem with overcrowding. Learning how to minimize the stressors in their coop, removing any aggressive and inured birds, and following the right lighting guidelines can make a big difference for how well this problem is solved.

Egg Eating

Sometimes, an egg can get broken inside the coop. Perhaps you were a little bit late cleaning out the eggs in the morning or the chickens laid at off times and it got broken up and smooshed. Sometimes, the hen is going to be interested in tasting this broken egg, and once the hen has tasted the egg, she will continue to eat broken ones, and even break open other eggs to eat at them. This could lead to a big mess inside of your coop that is hard to get under control. One of the best ways to keep the hens from eating the eggs is to prevent it from happening in the first place by keeping the coop cleaned up.

Chicken Mites

Roost mites are basically tiny bugs that can get on your chickens and drink their blood. If you don't check your chickens, these mites will be able to make your chickens sick and lead to death. You will first be able to notice if the mites are present by inspecting the eggs; if tiny red spots are on the eggs, you need to check whether mites are present. Another sign is the underside of the roosts or if your chickens are refusing to lay in their nest boxes since they will not do this if mites are present.

If you do have an infestation of the mites, it is a good idea to use permethrin, which is a good insecticide. You will also need to work hard to keep the chicken coop as sanitary as possible. Wood ashes and mite sprays can work too, but make sure to check these out with your vet before using.

Molting

Molting is not really a problem that you need to worry about, but as a new owner, it may seem like a huge issue. The hens are going to start looking bare and ragged and you may feel like there is some underlying health concern, but it is completely natural. Most chickens are going to go through the molting process about once each year, usually in the fall, but there are times when the molting process can happen two or more times.

The molting process is basically when the chicken looses their feathers before growing in new ones, often thicker ones that can help them to get through the weather. During this time, the chickens are not going to lay any eggs. The molting process will last 3 months, but there are some instances where it can take a bit longer. There is really nothing that you will be able to do to stop or prevent molting, just let it finish out the process.

Broody Hens

Hens will go broody when they want to hatch a nest of eggs, sit on them, and make sure that the eggs are getting the proper warmth. Even if there is no way that the eggs are fertilized, such as not having a rooster in the flock, the hen is not going to give you these eggs without causing a lot of fuss, including pecking and hissing. If you are looking to get some baby chicks to help replace the aging hens on your farm, you will want to get the hens to brood. On the other hand, if you would like to eat these eggs, a broody hen is going to be a nightmare.

If you would like to break up the broody hen, you will need to take her away from the rest of the flock. Keep her isolated from the rest of the flock, away from the nesting boxes, and just give her water and food. If this isn't working, you can use a clutch of ice cubes in the nest rather than the eggs to try and turn her away from doing this.

Lice

If you allow the chickens to use dust bathing and to preen on a regular basis, you most likely will not have to worry about a lice problem. Lice will live on chickens and eat their dead feathers and skin cells. They are often easy to cure and spot, but you should check the tail feathers and look to see if there is any white stuff that is getting stuck in the feather shafts. You can add on a dusting of a high quality lice powder to cure the issue, but make sure that you add this treatment to all of the chickens, not just the one you say the problem on, to ensure they are all going to be healthy.

Egg Bound

Some new backyard chicken farmers are curious to find out if their chickens are about to lay an egg. Maybe the chicken has gone a few days without any signs of laying an egg, but she is still heading to the nest box and is having trouble walking. This could mean that the chicken is egg bound. Some signs to look for when it comes to checking if you're chicken is egg bound includes:

- Drooping wings and getting lots of sleep
- Walking, stopping, and then straining to keep going,
- A sore and pulsating vent
- Feathers that are fluffed up
- Labored breathing

If you notice that these signs are present, it is likely that your chicken is egg bound. It is a good idea to fill up a buck of warm water or give the chicken a bath. You will need to lower the chicken slowly into this water, holding onto the wings so that they are not able to flap and make a mess. This can help the chicken to relax, but you should leave her in the bath for a minimum of twenty minutes, making sure that the water stays warm.

After the bath, you should keep the hen warm, dry her off, and then let her go back to her box for a few hours. Often the warm water will have helped to relax the vent a little bit and she will be able to pass along the egg in no time.

Being Careful Around Chickens

While there are many ways that your chickens can get sick, there are also some simple habits that you will be able to ensure that your chickens are staying healthy and that you are not getting sick from the chickens as well. Some of the tips that you should follow for this include:

- Washing your hands—no matter where you go, it is a good idea to clean your hands. Any time that you have fed the chickens, worked in their coop, handled the chickens, or collected the eggs, you should make sure to wash your hands with warm water and soap when you are done.
- Wear a face mask—there is going to be a lot of dust that is kicked around by your chickens. If the coop is enclosed,

make sure to wear a face mask of some sort. This helps to keep the dust and some of the bacteria in the air out of your body and if you're sick, it can prevent these pathogens getting into the chickens.

- Misting with water—using a light mist with water can help to reduce the dust that is around. You do not want to soak the area because this can create mud, but just a little mist, even with a little bleach to clean out the coop, can help to cut down on bacteria and clears the dust.
- Always clean the coop—most of these medical issues with your chickens are going to occur because you are not taking good care of the coop. Try to clean up at least once a week, including sweeping out the coop and dusting down as much as possible.
- Wear different clothing with the chickens—when you get out into the coop, you could get a lot of dust and other substances in your clothing. Consider having a special pair of clothing that you wear with the chickens. This helps to prevent you from spreading materials to the chickens and keeps the chicken materials out of your life.
- Observe the flock—one of the best ways to ensure that you are catching any issues with the flock is to pay attention. If you start to notice that something is off, get it checked out. If you notice that one of the birds looks sick, move them away from the rest of the flock so that they don't get anyone else

sick. It is much easier to take care of the birds and get them the right help when you are paying attention.
- Have a special pair of coop shoes—you don't want to bring in your regular shoes to the coop. First, these may not have the right amount of support and traction to keep you save inside the coop. Second, do you really want to track in your dirt and grime from the coop to your home?
- Watch your children around the chickens—it is never a good idea to leave your children around the chickens without supervision. If there are aggressive roosters around, the children can be harmed. If the children touch their mouths or cough on the chicken or something similar, you may notice that the chickens can get sick.
- Wash the eggs—it is always a good idea to wash off your eggs before you eat them. Even if you leave them in the fridge, it can be a nice precaution to wash them off first. This helps to take away all the dirt and other bacteria that could get onto the eggs before you eat them.
- Keep chickens isolated—it is never a good idea to introduce foreign birds and visitors to the chickens very often. This is one of the quickest ways to introduce disease to the chickens. You shouldn't share equipment and tools with other chicken owners either because this can spread disease as well.

While these steps may seem unnecessary and like you are having to take a lot of precautions that are only wasting your time, they are critical to keeping your flock healthy as well as keeping your family healthy. Make sure to stick with these tips for the long term and you can have one of the best flocks in the area!

Chapter 6: Making Money With Your Chickens

Many people decide to bring chickens into their home because it is a great project to enjoy with their family. It can help to teach your children how to be a bit more responsible, brings the family the opportunity to hang out and bond together, and can even provide you with some fresh eggs and meat that are way cheaper than what you can find at the store.

While these are all great reasons to get started on raising chickens in your backyard, it is also popular to raise these chickens in order to make some money. There are many different ways that your chickens can help you to make some extra money on the side, even if you have a tiny backyard, as long as you are willing to put in the time and the effort.

Selling the Eggs

One of the easiest things that you can do to make money from your new chicken farm is to sell the eggs. Even a few hens are going to be able to lay quite a few eggs and you may find that with a whole flock, you are not able to keep up with all of the eggs that are being produced. Whether you keep a few for yourself or you want to make a complete profit from all the eggs that come out of your chickens, you will find this is a relatively easy way to make some money.

First you will need to determine how many chickens that you will like to have. Keep in mind that each chicken is going to lay an egg every 1 to 2 days. This means with a flock of 15 hens, you could end up with more than 100 eggs each week if they are really getting to work. For the relatively low cost of getting started and for how much people are willing to pay for farm fresh eggs, you may be able to turn a tidy profit after the coop is all set up.

Of course, the more hens you have around, the more eggs you will be able to sell. But you have to keep in mind the amount of room that is available in your backyard. The hens will not produce well if you keep too many in one place and you may need to separate out the flocks into different coops. If you have a large farm, you may be able to keep quite a few chickens in the area, but for smaller backyards, you will be stuck with just a few hens.

Sell the Baby Chickens

Having your own hens can have many benefits. One is that when you add in the rooster, you can often get fertilized eggs that will grow into little baby chickens. Of course, you can choose to eat these fertilized eggs, but if you are looking for another source of income, it may be wise to consider letting these fertilized eggs become hatched. There are a lot of small scale farmers who would love to have these baby chicks to star their own backyard chicken farms and you could be the one to provide this to them.

This can sometimes be done slowly. For example you may start out having a few chickens in your backyard to get some fresh eggs or to have as a family pet and then later on decide to fertilize some of the eggs and let them hatch. Even a few chickens every other month or so can turn a nice profit without a ton of work on your part.

You will need to bring in an incubator to help with this process. This can help to keep the eggs nice and warm, even if the mother hen doesn't want to sit on them all day long; though you should make sure to go through and allow a brooding hen to do the work if possible. You can then decide to keep a few of the chicks to replenish some of your aging flock or to sell them off by word of mouth or at flea markets. Remember that you are only going to need one rooster for every ten or so hens so it can be really affordable.

Raising for Meat

There is nothing better than the taste of fresh off the farm chicken meat, and if you are raising chickens in your own backyard, this can be a daily reality for you. There are a lot of backyard farmers who will simply keep the meat for themselves. This allows them the opportunity to have fresh meat for a fraction of the cost that they get at the grocery store any time that they want. But if you are looking for a way to make some extra money, raising the chickens and then selling them as fresh meat can be a great option.

There are quite a few people out there who are willing to pay good prices for free range chicken. If you raised your chickens outside and allowed them to wander most of the day and come and go as they pleased, even if they were limited to a single area, you have free range chicken. Even those who aren't into the whole free range idea will love the idea of having fresh chicken available to them all of the time.

Before you sell the chickens for meat though, make sure to check out the local laws in your area. There are some areas that are pretty lax on these kinds of things but others are really strict and can place a lot of limitations on what you are allowed to do. If you talk to your local agricultural extension agent as well as the county health department, you will get a good idea on the rules and what you need to do in order to sell the chicken meat.

If you are selling chicken meat for a profit, you need to make sure that you keep the flock up. One choice is to continue purchasing birds and maturing them before butchering, but this is going to add to your overall cost. A better option is to allow fertilized eggs to hatch and then allow these chickens to grow up to be butchered. You can keep a few hens back each season to replace the aging birds and never have to spend more to bring more chickens into the flock.

Composted Manure

Now this is one of the ideas that a lot of people are not going to think about when they first get started with raising chickens, but you can actually make some money simply by saving the composted manure that your chickens are leaving all over the place. The bedding and manure that are already found in the chicken coop, and which may take you some time to clean up, can often be sold to local gardeners to help them get better fruits and vegetables. It doesn't have to take a lot of your time and will turn around a little extra money each month.

Before getting started on this process, you may want to read up a bit to learn how to take care of the manure. The composting process does not have to be difficult and since you are already removing all of this from the chicken coop in the first place, you already have a good start. Learn how to go through the composting process to get the best results and to sell a superior product to your customers.

Write About Your Experience

If you have been doing the backyard chicken raising, or any self-sustaining lifestyle, you may be able to make a profit writing about it or sharing your knowledge with others. There are quite a few people who are interested in learning how to live off the grid or at least save some money by growing a good garden and taking care of chickens by themselves. They would love to get this information first hand from someone who has done all the work and knows how to make it all fit together. If you have a knack for speaking to other people or you like to write, this could be a good career choice for you.

While most people get into the idea of raising chickens in their backyards because it is easy and affordable and provides them with tasty eggs and meat while bonding with their families, there is nothing wrong with taking some time to learn how to make money from all this work. Whether you want to turn this into a full time job or just add a little extra income to your life, raising chickens can be a great way to add to your income!

Conclusion

Raising chickens in your backyard can be one of the best ways to start out a life of self-sufficiency and to take care of yourself without relying on the big department stores. There is nothing better than putting in a little bit of hard work while spending time with your family and getting fresh eggs and meat for hardly any money out of the process. You don't need to have a lot of room at home to get this process started and even just a few hens will be enough to make it worth your time.

This guidebook has taken the time to look through all the different aspects that you need to know in order to see some success in raising chickens. Whether you have a smaller space or quite a bit of room, you will find a lot of enjoyment when it comes to raising chickens for yourself. From learning how to pick out the right breed for your family to choosing the right food, making the coop, and ensuring that you or the chickens don't get sick, this guidebook is ready to help you get started!

Homesteading
A Beginners Guide To Homesteading
Nancy Ross

Table of Contents

Introduction

Chapter 1: The Basics of Homesteading

Chapter 2: Raising Your Own Livestock in Your Backyard

Chapter 3: The Magic of Gardening for Your Own Food

Chapter 4: Preserving Your Food for Winter

Chapter 5: Making Your Own Clothes and Household Items

Conclusion

Introduction

The homestead movement has been around for years and is slowly gaining in popularity. People who are tired of being at the mercy of their local stores in terms of products available and prices are finding that the simplicity and hard work of living in the homestead movement is perfect for them. This is a movement that allows us to go back to our roots, think back to the 1800s when people basically had to fend for themselves for a lot of the things they needed.

The modern homestead movement is a little bit different than what you would find back in the 1800s, but the ideas are still the same. Ideally, you would be able to go out to your own acreage and take care of everything yourself, without having to get food, clothing, water or electricity or anything else from another source. Of course, this is a little bit difficult for a lot of people to accomplish; some don't want to give this much commitment, at least in the beginning, and others may like their current lifestyles and just want to save some money. This is why the definition of homesteading has changed over the course of time to include anyone who is working towards a life of self-sufficiency, even those who aren't all the way there yet.

This guidebook is going to provide you with all of the information that you need to understand the homestead lifestyle and what you will need to do in order to get started. Whether you are just looking to give a few of the aspects a try and want to know where to get started or you would like to jump all in and live this lifestyle to the fullest, this guidebook has the information that you need to get started.

The homestead lifestyle has so many benefits that you are going to be able to enjoy. The simplicity of life, the ability to only rely on yourself and your neighbors and even the chance to just sit back and enjoy the more important things in life, such as your family, can make the homesteading lifestyle all worth it. Read through this guidebook and learn all the important things that you need in order to get started, whether big or small, on the homesteading lifestyle.

Chapter 1: The Basics of Homesteading

The world is full of many amazing technological advances. We are used to hearing all about the latest and greatest that was invented to help make lives easier and to help us interact with other people. We go to the grocery store or a fast food restaurant to get all of our food. We go to the department store to get our clothes or any other household items that we may need. We also have to rely on the utility companies to supply us with our basic energy needs.

All of this may have made life easier, but it has certainly made us dependent on other people and may cost us quite a bit. Many people are getting tired of all this dependency. They don't like that they are forced to pay high prices for items to make a company rich when they could make the same items at home. Out of this frustration came the whole idea of homesteading.

Homesteading is an idea of becoming self-sufficient. It is the realization that you are able to do a lot of these tasks, such as raise your own food, make your own homemade products, and even grow a garden to help you get by. Now, there are varying degrees of homesteading. Some people may choose to grow a few vegetables and raise some chickens in their backyard to create a little bit of self-sufficiency while others will go all the way and never rely on department or grocery stores ever again because they can do all the work on their own.

There is no right or wrong answer when it comes to homesteading. Every little bit is a big step to protecting our earth and helping you to save money. While the term is meant more towards those who go back to the roots of homesteading and can provide everything for themselves, the whole movement realizes that some people may not be able to do this. If you work a full time job and are rarely home, or live in an apartment building, you may not be able to grow all the food that you need, make your clothes, and provide your own energy source. But the idea is to reduce the human impact on the environment and to stop relying on the ups and down of corporate America to provide us with these basic necessities.

The History of Homesteading

To get a better idea of the homesteading movement, let's take a look at some of the history that comes with homesteading. During the 1800s, homesteading became a popular term thanks to the Homesteading Act of 1862. This act basically provided land grants of up to 160 acres to any adult citizen. You would need to pay a small fee to register and then live on the land for five continuous years. After this time, you were given the deed to this land and could do what you would like with it.

This was mainly to encourage people to go out and start living in the western parts of the country. Those who had never stood a chance of owning their own land would flock out to these areas for practically free land and set up their own farms and families in that area. It was widely popular and allowed many people to own the farms they held for years.

This program technically ended in 1976 thanks to the Federal Land Policy and Management Act, but it started to end in 1935 when President Roosevelt began his conservation programs by using public domain lands. During the years that it was available, more than 783,000 men and women moved out to these areas and made it the five years to keep the land for themselves.

Back to the Land

After the Homestead Act was officially over, the term homesteading began to take a change. It was during the 1970s that this term started to evolve into what it means today. Homesteading is now more of a way to leave the modern conveniences of life behind you and returning to more rural roots. Tens of thousands of young adults as well as those with a bit of adventure in them decided to leave the suburbs and big cities in order to go back out into the country and start to take care of things for themselves. This continued to be a trend for the next thirty years and started to include those who were trying to live self-sufficiently even while living in a city as well as those who were in rural areas.

Modern Homesteading

The modern definition of homesteading is all about being self-sufficient. The ideal is to be self-sufficient in every aspect including providing your own food, making your own clothes, and providing everything that you need without help from outside sources other than from perhaps a few neighbors. Of course, providing this self-sufficiency takes a lot of time and patience and not everyone is able to take this kind of commitment, which is why all forms of self-sufficiency are welcome in this definition.

Even if you are only able to raise a few chickens and grow a small garden, you are taking the right steps to doing homesteading. Many people start out with these simple steps and find out that they love the homesteading so much that they will continue on until they are completely self-sufficient. Others decide this is all they have time for and that is perfectly fine as well. The main idea is to decrease the dependency that you have on modern conveniences and the big corporate world and instead go back to your roots and enjoy the simpler things in life.

Sometimes people are turned off by the idea of homesteading because they think they will need to jump into the lifestyle 100% or else they can't be a part of it. While some people relish the idea of owning their own farm and raising all their meat and food while also taking care to make their own clothes and furniture and live completely off the grid, this just isn't possible for others. Some people may not want to live this kind of lifestyle for some reason or another or it just isn't possible for them at the time.

You do not have to go off the grid and completely abandon society in order to be a part of this movement. Every little thing that you can do to change your habits and lifestyle to become a little more self-efficient will help you to join this movement. Thinking about growing your own garden and having some produce ready in the fall to save time and money? This is a part of the homesteading movement. Thinking about learning how to make your own beauty products such as shampoos and soaps at home? This is a part of the homesteading movement as well. While the original ideas behind this movement were more geared towards living off the grid and only getting help from your friends and neighbors, it is now a movement that embraces anyone who would like to gain some independence from the modern lifestyle.

Anyone is able to join this kind of movement and all you need is some determination to succeed and a little bit of good work ethic to keep on going. Once you learn a few new tricks along the way, you will find that the homestead lifestyle can be a great one to enjoy.

Benefits of Homesteading

Homesteading can sometimes be a lot of hard work. You have to take on the work that usually is done by someone else in order to gain that self-sufficiency that you always dreamed about. But with all of the benefits that come with homesteading, it is a wonder that more people don't decide to jump on board. Here are some of the biggest benefits that you can enjoy from homesteading and why you should consider this lifestyle with your family.

Builds a Good Work Ethic

Nothing is going to be better for a good work ethic than homesteading. Getting your family started on this kind of lifestyle early can help to build a good work ethic. When you go all out with homesteading, there is going to be a lot of work for everyone to accomplish. You have to take care of the animals, grow a big garden, learn how to sew and knit, keep the home clean, prepare beauty and cleaning products, canning, butchering, and so much more. Everyone is going to have to get to work and contribute if everyone wants to succeed.

Now, some parents may think this is a bad thing to put your kids to work in the homesteading lifestyle, but it is teaching kids so many valuable lessons. As long as you are giving each child a task that is suitable for their age level, such as helping to plant seeds and keeping their rooms clean for younger children, they are going to learn the benefits of hard work without any negatives happening to them.

More Time to be with Family

If you choose to go with the full homesteading experience, you will be able to spend a lot more time with your family. Most people who do homesteading completely are going to give up their regular jobs and instead focusing on this kind of lifestyle. Even if you are still keeping your regular job, all the work that needs to be done for homesteading will allow you and your family to spend some quality time together.

In between feeding the animals, growing the garden, making your clothes and household items, and all the other things that you will need to do, you are sure to get plenty of time with your family. You won't have to miss out so much on your kids growing up or worry about them spending too much time in front of the television. It is great getting to spend time with your family and homesteading can be one of the best ways to get started on this.

The modern world is too full of being busy all of the time. In between working a full time job or two, going to school, and all of the after school sports activities and time visiting with friends, it doesn't take long before you miss out on that valuable time seeing your kids grow up. In addition, most of the time that you are spending at home may be spent in front of a computer screen or television screen, or even doing homework. This is time that is wasted and you are missing out on those important years.

This is why homesteading can be so important. Even with just raising a few chickens or working on a garden, you are at least coming up with a way that the whole family can work on something together. You should schedule out time when everyone needs to be out and working on these homesteading projects, time that you aren't allowed to work on anything else or have other activities scheduled. This will help you to really spend time with one another and perhaps reduce some of the stress that you are all feeling.

If you do choose to go with the whole homesteading experience, you may even choose to go with homeschooling your children to reduce their dependence on modern lifestyle choices even more. This can be a great way to spend some more time with your children and to help them to learn in a way that is best for them. You won't lose out on that precious day time with the kids while they are at school, you can all work on supporting the family together, and they will learn so much more than they would ever be able to in the classroom.

Tastes Better

Food that is grown at home is just going to taste so much better. The foods that you purchase the grocery store are often full of preservatives and other things that are going to change the taste so much. Even the fresh produce has had ingredients added to help them last a little bit longer on the shelves. Nothing is going to taste better than being able to go out to your own garden, pick some fruits and vegetables, and have them on your plate for dinner that night.

Think of it this way; have you ever gone out to a farm and been able to bite into a tasty strawberry picked straight from the vine? Or have you ever had someone bring one of the most delicious salads ever from their own backyard garden? These people are practicing at least a form of the homesteading lifestyle and you could get all these great flavors added to your table if you just got started.

Rewarding

Homesteading can be one of the most rewarding things that you will do with your life. Think of how great you will feel after you eat a meal that is full of fresh chicken as well as fresh fruits and vegetables from your garden. Think of how proud you will be seeing your kids learn how to make their own toys or wearing that outfit that you just learned to sew. It is one thing to be able to run to the department store or grocery store and pick up the things that you need, but it is something else completely when you are able to do all the work yourself.

There is nothing more rewarding than being able to create your own household items. Many people worry that this will be too hard, but you only need to start with one or two things at a time. As you learn more and get better at your current skills, you will find that learning something else is not impossible. Even with the little things, you will soon be able to look around at your handiwork and feel how rewarding it is to put in a hard days' work.

Less Dependency on Others

One of the main reasons that a lot of people will choose to go into homesteading is because they are tired of being dependent on others. Perhaps they are tired of having to pay such high prices at the store each month in order to feed their families. Some people are worried that a natural disaster, or the government, could quickly shut down their food supplies and they will be stuck with nothing if they don't get started on homesteading. Whether you are concerned about these issues or are more interested in just being able to count on yourself, homesteading can be a great way to make this happen.

And this is the root of the homesteading movement. It is the idea that we are too dependent on the modern world, a world that is fragile and could fall apart with a natural disaster or a change in government in another country. When we start to take these tasks and do them ourselves, we are certain that we are always taken care of rather than hoping that things do not go south at some point.

Everyone goes into homesteading for different reasons. Some want to learn how to connect with nature and spend more time with their kids and others just like the idea of being able to rely solely on themselves and not the big stores. No matter your reason for getting into homesteading, it can be a really rewarding adventure.

Chapter 2: Raising Your Own Livestock in Your Backyard

The first aspect of homesteading that we will take a look at is the livestock. Livestock can be a great way to create your own meat to enjoy all throughout the year and there are options no matter how much room you have to spare. If you are lucky enough to have an acreage, you may be able to include some bigger livestock such as cows. Others may be limited to their own backyard so they may choose to have something small and easy like chickens. No matter which one you choose to go with, you are making some great strides with homesteading!

Chickens

Raising chickens can be a great experience. Most chickens do not need a ton of space to live as long as you allow them a little room to roam during the day and a safe place to call home at night. One male chicken to every ten to fifteen female chickens is enough to keep the fresh eggs coming and to help ensure that your flock continues to grow with the fertilized eggs. You can also choose to just have female chickens if you are just interested in the meat and the eggs without growing the flock.

Chickens are relatively easy to take care of as long as you keep the coop clean, prevent them from getting sick or starting fights, and provide them with healthy and delicious food. They are great for a lot of good fresh meat and you can expect some fresh eggs every day or two to help feed your family.

There are a number of ways that you are going to be able to enjoy chickens on your homestead. First, they work really well as pets for the family and can teach some responsibility to your children without taking up all that much space. If you have a backyard and can fence it in a little bit, the chickens are going to be just fine. You will need to give them some room to roam and make sure to clean out the coop and collect the eggs, but for the most part, the chickens will take care of the majority of the work.

You will also be able to use the chickens to get a steady stream of food. You can use their eggs each day to help out with your breakfast for a much lower cost than they are in the grocery store. You will also be able to butcher some of the chickens at the end of the year and freeze the meat to enjoy on your dinner table. If you would like to keep your costs down even more, you may consider hatching a few of the eggs and letting them grow up, rather than eating all the eggs, so you have a constant source of fresh meat and fresh eggs without having to pay for more chickens.

Goats

Another animal that you may want to consider when homesteading are goats. It is often best to get started with just one or two goats to see how this is going to work out for your needs. Sometimes goats can be a handful and it is better to find out that you are not fond of having them around when you only have two rather than finding this out with a whole herd in your backyard.

Goats can be a wonderful option to have in your backyard homestead. You will be able to drink the ultra healthy goat milk throughout the year and the meat is really healthy for your body and can fill you up for a long time. Before making the purchase of a goat, make sure that you have enough land to raise them, and pay special attention to the fences that you have in place. You will need to have some kind of fence, whether it is an electric fence or some traditional form of fence, to keep the goats in place. You can also consider a holding pen for those times you need to give the goats vaccination.

When purchasing a goat, make sure to go with a reputable seller who is able to provide you with the background of each goat that you purchase. Many new homesteaders are interested in going with a sale barn because of the prices, but you will have no idea the background of your goats and this can be dangerous for you and for the goat. You want to make sure that the goat does not have any diseases or need special care before bringing them home.

You may want to consider having at least one buck along with several does for the goats or have a means to get in touch with a buck at some time. This can help you to breed easier and you can keep on more goats for less cost down the road or sell them to make a little bit of profit.

Taking care of goats can be a little bit of a challenge. You need to make sure that they have plenty of room to roam and a lot of food to eat or they can get into trouble. Again, that fence can be a nice addition because it ensures that they are staying in place and not getting into the trash, garden, or other areas where you would rather they stay away. Make sure to do your research on the different kinds of goats to find the one that is right for you and to understand what raising goats entails.

Pigs

Another option that you can choose if you have the room is to raise your own pigs. Pigs don't take a ton of work to take care of and that tasty meat can make all the difference when winter arrives and you don't need to go to the grocery store. If you live in town though, make sure to check with your local ordinances to see what the rules are for having pigs in the neighborhood.

Pigs can often thrive as grazing animals, though it is a good idea to add some variety to their diets including extra milk and whey and garden and food scraps as well. The pigs will use their own rooting instincts can help them to find even more of the food that they need to do well and you can put these animals to work with helping on the farm once you get used to them.

Most homesteaders will choose to have pigs around because of all the amazing meat that they can get. Think about the sausages, bacon, pork chops and more that you can get out of pigs without having to pay the high prices at the store and without having to worry about the inhumane ways that many big farms treat their livestock. Just a few pigs can be enough to fill up that deep freezer and get you set all winter.

Pigs can be valuable for more than just their meat, although this is an important aspect as well. Many farmers keep pigs around to help out with their gardening and other chores around the homestead. For example, the compost from the pigs can be really rich in nutrients and will make that garden grow like crazy. Bring the pigs out into the garden to help mix the compost into the dirt and you are going to have a better crop then ever before. Make sure to reward the pigs with some tasty corn as a treat.

Cows

And of course, raising cows is a great way to get a lot of meat and milk that you need to become self-sufficient. You just need to make sure that you have the space to make this happen. Unlike chickens and goats, you will not be able to fit the cows into your own backyard, so finding a larger area, or going with one of the other animals, may be the choice that you need. But if you have the room and the time, raising cows can be well worth the effort.

Cows can provide a number of benefits to your homestead. You can keep the cows happy on your farm and get milk from them every day, a luxury that can get really expensive at the local grocery store. You can allow the cows to roam around on the homestead and eat up some of the weeds and grass that would get out of hand otherwise to keep the homestead looking great. And at the end of the season, you can choose to butcher a few of the cows to use them as meat to make it through the winter. Think of how tasty it will be to have some of your own fresh milk and fresh meat available whenever you want.

As mentioned, your cows are going to need a little bit of space to live. If you would like to have the cows graze, you will need two acres or so for each cow. You can also raise them in a feedlot area if you're short on space and then just provide them with concentrated feed and roughage to keep them big and strong. You can also choose to place the cows in half of the pasture and have it gated up and switch them over to the other half to give the grass a break and still allow the cows some room to wander around.

Make sure to be careful with the fencing that you are providing to your cows because some types may cause external harm to the cows. Providing them with enough water each day, somewhere between twelve and twenty gallons every day, can help them to stay hydrated and not get sick. These animals are going to take a bit more time to raise and take care of, but compared to the cost of beef and milk at the store, you are going to get an amazing deal and won't have to rely on the grocery stores.

These are just a few of the types of animals that you may be considering adding to your homestead adventure. These animals can make life easier, providing you with eggs, milk, and meat to last all year long and keep you healthy for a fraction of the cost of purchasing at the store. Make sure to learn how much space each animal needs and whether you have the time available to give them everything that they need for the best results.

Chapter 3: The Magic of Gardening for Your Own Food

If you are just starting to consider homesteading but are concerned about having the right amount of time or energy to really get into the whole idea, it may be good to start with some basic gardening. Even a small garden with just a few plants can be the start of homesteading as it allows you just a tiny bit of self-sufficiency. You can start out small and slowly build up so that most of your produce and herbs come from your own garden. Who knows, perhaps you will love this process so much that you will turn all the way into homesteading with the other great ideas.

Starting your Garden

Starting your garden can be a great process. You will first need to figure out where you would like to place the plants. The best spot is going to be in an area you can see. If you never see the plants, it is going to be really hard to remember and stay motivated to take care of the garden and soon it will all go to ruins. So first pick out a spot that is easy to see from your back windows so you are always reminded to take care of the plants.

Next, you need to pick an area in your garden that will get plenty of sunlight. There are many areas that may get too much shade due to the angle of the home to the ground and you want to avoid these as much as possible. Your plants need to take in as much sunlight as possible so pick a place that is going to bring on that sun. This place also needs to have the ability to get a lot of rain to the plants. While you may need to water the plants on occasion, the rain water is usually the best. So basically make sure that you pick a spot that is not shaded from the sun or close to a tree.

The soil quality of your area is going to make a difference as well. You want to provide your plants with soil that is full of nutrients and will help them to grow big and strong. If you haven't taken care of your yard for some time, you may want to consider tilling up the soil to allow some oxygen to get inside and then mix in a good potting soil to get some extra nutrients mixed in for the plants.

Choosing Your Plants

Once the area is picked out and prepared, it is time to choose the plants that you would like to work with. If this is your first time ever creating a garden, it is probably best to stick with just one or two plants that will provide you with some great food. You may be excited to get started with this process and want to go all out, but this can end up being a lot of work and if you're not properly ready, you may want to give up on the whole mess.

Tomatoes are a good choice to start with. They are really sturdy and there are a lot of great canning recipes that you can choose to go with to really make things easier. Peas and carrots and corn work out well too or maybe you would like to try out a few herbs or a little bit of fruit to make things interesting. The choice is up to yours, just pick out fruits and vegetables that are easy to grow that first year and that you are willing to eat.

Over time, you will be able to increase the amount of vegetables and fruits that you are growing and maybe someday you will grow a garden that is big enough to feed the entire family. That is a great goal to have, but start out small and get used to the idea before you jump in and get over your head.

When you're trying to figure out the plants that you would like to add into the garden, think of the foods that you like to add to your plate at dinner time. The ones that make your mouth water and help you to feel good when you eat them fresh. These are the produce choices that you should make first to ensure that you are putting in the hard work for the food that you will actually eat.

Designing Your Garden

There are different designs that you can choose to do with your garden that can help make it easier and more fun to handle. Some people may need to go with a certain design because it fits into their backyards a little bit better while others may be interested in having a design to keep certain products together. The choice is up to you, but decide on the design of the garden before you start planting.

Often, it is a good idea to draw out the design that you would like to use each year. You do not want to continue growing the same crop in the same place each year. This is simply going to dry up the soil and after a few years, your plants are going to start wilting and having some trouble growing because they aren't getting the nutrition that they need. And remembering where you put the crops from year to year can become a challenge so writing out the diagram can help you keep things in order.

You can make a choice when it comes to designing your own personal garden. You may just take a square and put like together with like to make things easier. Others may be interested in making this garden look appealing and will create a masterpiece. Even considering putting it up a little so you don't have to bend all of the way down to the ground can help make the gardening process easier.

The size of your garden can make a big difference on how you will design it. Smaller gardens may not be able to hold as much in terms of produce, but you can be smart and plan things out to hold quite a few crops. Consider planting all your fruits and vegetables in straight lines and then adding some herbs in between to really utilize the space and get the most out of your small area. On the other hand, if you have a lot of room, such as moving to an acreage, you may find that it is easier to grow enough crops to take care of your family all year round without having to go to the local market.

Finding the Right Tools

Gardening does not have to be complicated and having a few tools on hand can help you to get it all done right. Some of the options that you should keep on hand for your garden include:

- Shovel—no garden is complete without having a shovel to dig holes, get rid of the weeds, and even to help till up some of the soil. You can consider having a few varieties in size to get the best results.
- Pruners—at times, some part of your plant may start to die out. This does not mean that the whole plant has to go though. You can choose to use some pruners to cut off some of the dead stuff and keep the plant growing strong.
- Pots—some plants can be done completely in the garden and others may need a little head start in a pot. In addition, you may find that growing a garden inside can be enjoyable and easier if you live in the city and you will need pots to accomplish this.

- Watering can—while rain water is always the best for plants, you can't always rely on the rain to come when you most need it. Having a watering can to transport the water to the garden can make things a little easier.
- Trowel—this can be helpful when it's time to prepare the garden. Rake this through the soil a few times to help loosen things up and get more nutrients to the plants. It also works well for getting rid of some of those tough weeds.

Maintaining the Garden

Once all the crops are in place, you need to take the proper steps to maintain the garden, otherwise your hard work up to this point is going to end up worthless. First, you need to make sure that you are watering the plants at regular intervals. If it is raining often in your area, you may not need to go out and do this as much, but for those dryer periods of the year, it becomes your job to take care of the plants. A good way to tell if the plants need some more water is to feel the soil; if it feels dry to the touch, it is time to water your plants.

You should always monitor the pH of your garden. You want to have the right amount of each major nutrient in the soil for optimal growth. When you use a pH system, you will be able to tell how good the pH is in the ground and make the right adjustments. Adding in some more supplements to the soil can really make a difference in how well the plants are growing.

And finally, you have to take the time to weed. Weeding can be a pain and takes a lot of time, but as your plants grow, so do the weeds. You need to keep up on these otherwise the weeds are going to get out of control and they will start taking nutrients out of the soil and away from your plants. Check on the weeds ever week or so and you will find the job is not so complicated.

Maintenance of the garden is not always the most fun process, but you will find that it creates some of the best fruits and vegetables, as well as herbs, to help you to be ready for winter. Set up a schedule for taking care of the wedding, pruning the dead parts of the plant so it doesn't start to take away nutrients from the rest of the plant, and check the pH levels of the soil on occasion, adding in some more nutrients if the plant needs it. This will ensure that you get the very best produce every year.

Growing a garden does not have to be a complicated process, but rather an enjoyable one. Figure out how much you are going to be able to handle in the garden each year and keep up on the maintenance and you will find that your garden can be a really rewarding process.

Chapter 4: Preserving Your Food for Winter

Homesteading is meant to help you be self-sufficient in your whole life, not just in the summer and fall months. But for those who live in colder climates, it may be hard to imagine how you are going to be able to keep up with everything once it gets too cold to grow a garden or the animals are not able to produce as much milk and so on. Preserving your food is going to be key in this process and this chapter is going to take some time to discuss the different preservation methods that you can use to make that food last all year long.

While all of these types of preservation can be great for keeping your food healthy and delicious for a long time, you need to make sure that you are preparing and storing them properly. For example, if you are canning and don't ensure that a seal is completely met, you will find that the food can still spoil. You may need to experiment with some smaller batches ahead of time to get used to the idea before continuing to get the best results.

Canning

Canning is one of the most popular methods that you can use to preserve your food for the winter. It doesn't have to be complicated, just throwing together a few ingredients and sealing the jars just right can really help you to see the results that you are looking for. But it is really important that you get the ingredients prepared right, learn how to get the jars to close properly, and to store all the food in the correct locations if you would really like the food to stay good through the year.

There are two main ways of canning, the boiling water method and the pressure canning method. The boiling water method is best for preserves, pickles, jellies, jams, fruits, and tomatoes while the pressure canning is going to be the best for seafood, poultry, meats, and vegetables. Both are going to use water, but the pressure canning will go into higher temperatures and rely more on the pressure, rather than the heat, to help the foods get tight and secure in their jars.

To get started, you will need to find the right tools to make it happen. You will need to pick out some jars, usually Ball or Mason jars are the best along with the lids and the little sealers that come with them. Jar lifters, funnels, a lid want, clean cloths, hot pads, spatula, and knives can all help you to get through this process a little bit easier.

From here, you need to find a recipe that you really like to use. This will help you to know what ingredients are needed to can and preserve any food that you would like. Make sure to get the cans to really seal up, allowing them some time to cool down on the counters to finish this process, so that the food stays fresh.

Store these cans in a cool and dry area until you are ready to use. It may be best to include some labeling information, such as the name of the ingredients inside and the date that you canned them, to ensure you are not getting a product that is old. Your basement up on some shelves can often be a good place to put the food so it is out of the way and still being safe from any water and heat that could ruin the work.

Freezing

Freezing can be a great way to keep your food safe and happy for later use. Almost any type of food will do well with freezing as long as you follow the proper procedures along the way. You can choose to freeze your fruits and vegetables for later, any of the meat that you butcher, and so much more. If you are interested in using the freezing method to keep the food good over the winter after all that hard work, follow these basic steps.

- Cool foods to room temperature—if you left the produce out in the sun or cooked up some of the food before freezing, you need to allow it to reach room temperature before freezing. This helps the food to freeze as uniformly as possible and can help to prevent spoilage. Plus, hot foods can warm up the freezer and cause damage to some of the other foods inside.

- Leave some room—when using covered containers, leave a little room for the food to expand. An inch between the top of the food and the lid is usually enough and ensures that the food can expand without breaking the container.
- Press the air out—any time that you are wrapping up foods or placing in plastic bags, make sure that all of the air gets out. This can help to prevent freezer burn from occurring.
- Invest in the right wrappings—if you would like to keep these foods frozen for the long term, go with options that are meant for the freezing process. This really does a great job at helping keep the foods fresh for longer.
- Label the food—include as much information as possible. The date, the name of the food, and even some preparation instructions can help you out. Always take out the oldest food first to prevent anything getting old.
- Never overload your freezer—while it may be tempting to stuff the freezer full, this can prevent the right air circulation from occurring. This will prevent the temperatures from staying right where it should and the frozen food could spoil.

Drying

Another option that you can choose is drying. This will help to take the moisture out of the foods so that the water doesn't attract mold or other bacteria that makes the food uneatable. Drying does take a little more time and is not as quick as some of the other methods, but it can work really well if you need to store foods for a long time or for options like meats. Some of the steps that you should follow when it comes to the drying process includes:

1. Select the best pieces for dehydration—when you use freezing or canning, it is fine to add in some of the lower quality foods, but in dehydration, this is really going to show up and can ruin the texture if the perfect produce is not picked. Choose options that are at their peak eating quality, ripe, and don't have a lot of bruises on them.
2. Prepare the food how you will serve them—once the foods are dehydrated, they are going to stay that way while they are eaten so prepare the foods at this time. For example, you can choose to take an apple and puree it to make a leather, cut it into rings, or even slice it, but decide at this point.
3. Keep the pieces uniform—all your pieces should be the same height and width, usually between 1/8 and ¼ of an inch. This helps them to dry at the same speed and can quicken up the process.

4. Wash the foods—if you are drying option like seedless grapes, berries, and herbs, make sure to wash them off before dehydrating.
5. Light colored vegetables and fruits can do well with some lemon juice or steaming before you dehydrate them. This can prevent them from browning in the process.
6. Select the drying method—there are a number of methods that you can choose. Some like to use their ovens while others will purchase a dehydrator to do this process. If you live in an area that get steady sun that is hot, you can even use the sun for this.
7. Learn when the product is done—each product is going to take different times to finish. You want to make sure that all the moisture is out of these foods or they will rot while you store them so give them the right amount of time.
8. Seal up the products properly. You want to make sure that they are in containers that won't allow moisture and will keep the food safe for a long time. You will also want to pack it in as tight as possible so that the food is not going to get affected by air pockets.
9. Store the food in an area that is dry, dark, and cool and keep it away from heat sources to help it stay fresh. Use this food within twelve months to ensure that it is the best quality and frequently check the food to see if anything has gotten wet.

And that is all there is to it. While the drying process can often extend for a whole day or more to properly get the food ready, it is a really great way to take care of the food you would like to save without making a lot of changes to the taste when everything is done.

Chapter 5: Making Your Own Clothes and Household Items

For those who would like to really get into the whole idea of homesteading and want to leave all the hassles of the modern world behind, there are so many other things that you will be able to work on all by yourself. From the clothing that you wear to the beauty supplies that you start making and even your furniture and cleaning supplies, you are going to love how much fun it is to dive right into these projects. They can even be fun to do if you're just starting out with homesteading and want to build up your confidence!

Making Your Own Clothes

The first thing that you can consider doing to get started on homesteading is to make your own clothes. All of us know how expensive it can be when it comes to purchasing clothes for the whole family. Even if you aren't sticking to the name brands, you could easily spend a couple hundred dollars to fashion out each of your kids for school and often they won't wear all of the clothes because they grow too fast. Doesn't this seem like a lot of money that you could put elsewhere rather than on buying clothes each month?

Luckily, there are a lot of options that you can take. Some people who may not be as much into the arts and crafts, or don't have the time to do it like they want, may choose to go to thrift stores and purchase their clothes. These are often cheaper, helps to reduce a lot of the waste that has happened in our society, and helps you to get away from those big department stores.

Now, if you want to be really into the whole idea of homesteading, you will need to make your own clothes. And for this to happen, you need to understand that the size of your wardrobe is going to go way down. You are not going to have time to make twenty pairs of jeans for each kid and fifty shirts, especially considering how fast they will grow and how much this can add up to over a year. Get used to the idea that your kids may have to re-wear their clothes when you are homesteading and stick with the basic amount that is needed. You can always clean the clothes so they look nice and fresh.

There are many great outlines that you can use to help make a dress or paints or a shirt. Find a pattern that you like the best and then just change the sizes to fit everyone in the family. You may have to do some measuring and the first few articles of clothing may look a little bit silly, but overall this can be a fun experience that saves you money and helps you reach the homesteading idea faster.

Making Your Own Beauty Supplies

Next on the list is to make some of your own beauty supplies. Makeup, facial cleansers, bath soaps, perfumes, and more can quickly get expensive. When it comes to some of the best smells that are allergen free or promoted by your favorite celebrity, you are going to spend way over your budget to look and smell nice. Many people have chosen to completely drop the products to save time and money. But if you are one of those people who like having these products in their lives, you don't have to give them up if you choose to go homesteading.

Making your own beauty supplies can actually be a lot of fun and will utilize all natural ingredients rather than those that are manufactured in a plant and could be unsafe in your home. You will love that there are endless varieties when it comes to making your own supplies and the cost is way lower than what the top brands will offer to you. If you have oily hair, dry skin, like a certain color of eyeshadow, or have any other preferences when it comes to your beauty look, you will be able to just make them all up and get a great look for a fraction of the price.

There are many recipes that you can find online or through books for the various beauty products that you want to make. Choose a few and get the ingredients, some of which, like the herbs, you can grow in your own garden. You are going to love the variety as well as how easy it is to make some of these products and you may never go back to store bought beauty products again.

Making Your Own Cleaning Supplies

Even when you live on a homestead, you will still need to keep your home clean. Whether your little homestead is in a tiny apartment, a regular home in the suburbs, or out on an acreage where you are taking the homesteading experience to a whole new level, you will find that all of these areas need to be cleaned at some point. From the dishes, to the toilet, to the floors, and everywhere that can get messy in a home, especially with the kids, you will need to find the right cleaning products for your needs.

There are many options to choose from when it comes to picking out cleaning products from the store, but have you ever taken the time to look at the ingredients that are on them? Most of these ingredients are hard to pronounce and the ones that you will recognize are so harmful to the body that it is amazing that you are still using them. Plus, since you have to get these at the store, they are taking away a bit from your self-sufficiency.

You can choose to make any and all of these products at home and many of them will need just a few ingredients to complete. While your regular cleaner at the grocery store may have twenty or more ingredients, you can make window washer cleaner with just vinegar and water. Many of the other recipes that you choose to use in your home may include just three or four ingredients to help disinfect the area and help it to smell good. These can be so much safer in your home and around your kids while still providing all the cleaning power that you need to make the home look amazing.

Building Your Own Furniture and Other Products

Another thing that you can do to help become a homesteader and increase your level of self-sufficiency is to learn how to make your own furniture. Even if you've never had experience with doing woodworking before, now is the perfect time to get started and you can always start off a little small and then build up to something big. For example, you could start out with a little end table and then move up to making a few chairs before creating your very own dining room table.

This can be a fun way to enjoy homesteading, but you may have to start out slowly if you've never done this kind of woodworking before. It takes a bit of patience, but it can be amazing to go into your home and seeing that you were able to create all of the furniture, as well as any other items that you need, and for a much better price than you would be able to get from any furniture store.

Of course, you can start out slowly and bring some of your old home items with you. It is not likely that you will be able to make all of the items that your home needs right out the door and you don't want to wait years for a bed while you try to learn the whole process. But as things start to break in your home or you would like an update, learn how to handle the updates yourself and things an be so much better!

There are many great books that you can read through to learn how to make some of these products all on your own. Learn how to make furniture with woodworking, some of your own plates with some ceramic or clay, or any other product that you could use. It may take you some time to learn how to do all of this stuff, but you are going to have a big sense of pride when you finally figure it all out!

Learning how to make your own household products can be a great experience. To be completely a part of the homesteading lifestyle, you need to learn how to be self-sufficient from anyone else, except perhaps a few neighbors who help you out and you help them when needed. This means no more grocery stores, department stores, or any other places where you can pick up the good premade and take them home. Of course, there are variations on this that you can follow and any sort of self-sufficiency, even if it is just starting your own garden in your backyard can be considered a part of the homesteading movement, but if you want to go all out for this movement, you will certainly need to learn how to make everything yourself.

While some of this can seem daunting at first, remember that you are able to take it a step at a time. Perhaps just start with a small garden and build up to raising some animals and then making your own household items. There are no right or wrong ways of doing the homestead movement as long as you learn to enjoy the lifestyle and decrease your dependence on consumer goods. Have fun during the process, learn something new, and enjoy life, and you are following this movement properly.

Conclusion

The homesteading movement has been gaining popularity for years and many people are still drawn to the ideas of living on their own and taking care of things without all the consumer goods that bog down current society. Getting its roots from the Homestead Act of 1962, the homestead movement still has a lot of fans who are ready to live simpler lives, save money, and not be so reliant on all the modern technology and other things that could be ruining our lives and making us grow distant from the people we love.

This guidebook is going to take some time to look over the ideas behind the homesteading movement. While the true homesteading movement asks people to completely give up their modern lifestyles in order to take care of everything by themselves, it has grown to recognize that you may need to make adjustments based on your current living situation and time. For example, if you are able to grow a little garden in your apartment and make a few cleaning supplies, you can still be considered a part of the homesteading movement even if you don't go all out with the idea.

If you are interested in living a simple life that allows you to enjoy the things that are important to you rather than being reliant on the big chain stores or all the consumer goods, the homesteading movement can be the right choice for you.

Mini Farming

Mini Farming for Beginners

Nancy Ross

Table of Contents

Introduction

Chapter 1: What is Mini Farming?

Chapter 2: Simple Tricks to Maximize Your Space

Chapter 3: Best Plants for Mini Farming

Chapter 4: Picking the Right Soil, Pest Control, and Taking Care of Weeds

Chapter 5: What Livestock Do Well with Mini Farming?

Chapter 6: Tips to Make Mini Farming Easier

Conclusion

Introduction

Mini farming is a great way for you to get back to nature and enjoy all the bounty that life has to offer. Many people who choose to go with mini farming are those who want a big farm of their own but who aren't able to find or afford a place and others just want to enjoy all that life has to offer in their current limited space and to lower their dependency on the modern world. No matter the reason that you choose to go with mini farming, it can be a great experience for the whole family.

This guidebook is going to take some time to look over mini farming and how you are going to be able to get started. We will take a look at all the different aspects of mini farming including why it is such a big movement, how to plan out the farm and get the most out of your limited space, which plants to grow, and even the best livestock to have on this limited amount of space. The process may seem overwhelming at first, but you are going to find it is a great way to bond with your family, grow some of your own foods, and have some fun.

When you are ready to get started with mini farming, take a look through this guidebook and learn everything that you need to know to do a great job and get the most out of even the smallest areas!

Chapter 1: What is Mini Farming?

The modern world is full of so much stuff. We can go to the grocery store and find foods that are from all over the world. We can go to department stores and find clothes, toys, and gadgets, many of which are meant to make life easier and some that are just there to be novelties and make the inventor some money. We can have people make our food, make our clothes, and we can find items that are there to help you out with anything and everything in life.

While this can seem like a nice thing to enjoy in life, it is actually going to cause a lot of problems. The fewer things we do on our own, the more we become dependent on others around us. When the store is out of a certain food, we have to live without it or make adjustments to our plans. So what would happen if your store all of a sudden ended up empty and doesn't have any products available? Would you be able to provide for your family or would you be scrambling around looking for ways to eat?

Many Americans are starting to see the unhealthy this relationship can be. While it is nice to be able to go to the store and just pick out the items that you need, many families would be in some trouble if they had to start fending for themselves on a moment's notice. There are many that feel it is time to take a step back and start taking care of ourselves rather than relying on the big grocery stores or other people to provide us with the basic necessities.

And from this idea came mini farming. Mini farming is the idea that you can be self-sufficient, at least a little bit, from the mainstream world, and take care of some of our own things. Whether you just decide to take on a little bit of gardening and make some of your own food or you go all out and learn how to be self-sufficient completely from the modern world, mini farming can be the right solution for you.

Mini farming is the best choice for anyone no matter how much room you have available. There are many individuals who feel they are not able to join farming or homesteading or any of these other ideas because they don't have an acre or more of farmland to use. While having all this space may seem like it makes things easier, and it can allow for a little more food production or larger livestock, you don't have to miss out on all the great stuff that self-sufficiency offers just because you are a bit more limited on space.

Mini farming can be done in your own backyard. As long as you have some space for a nice garden, or even doing gardening in your own home, and some livestock like chickens or pigs, you can join this movement. An area as small as ¼ of an acre can be enough to help you to get started. You may be amazed at how easy this whole process can be as well as how much fun! Starting out small can make it so much easier, gives you a taste of why these movements are so amazing, and can help you to reach that self-sufficiency goal you are looking for.

The Basics of Mini Farming

Mini farming can appeal to almost everyone. Some people get into mini farming because they have always dreamed of having an acreage and doing things on their own, but perhaps they aren't able to follow that dream right now and are making use of the space around them. Others may choose to start the self-sufficiency lifestyle and they like the idea of growing their own produce and even keeping a few animals in the backyard. Some may want to go completely self-sufficient with the backyard farming and others just like having fresh from the garden foods and will get started with the mini farming.

No matter the reason you get started with mini farming, there are so many ways that you can go about the process. Let's take a look at the different things you should consider before getting started with mini farming.

Planning

The first thing that you will need to do to start with your mini farm is to plan it all out. Draw up a plan of your backyard or the area that you would like to use for your farm. You can take some time to watch the backyard, noticing which places get full sun, the parts that are in the shade part of the day, and then those that are going to be mostly shaded. These are going to make a big difference in where you place all of your plants.

Once you know where the sun is located in relations to your backyard, it is easier to plan out where you will put everything. You will be able to put the plants in an area that will get sun most of the day and move a shed over to someplace that is shaded most of the day and wouldn't be good for a garden. You may need to mess around with the plan a bit, but it's much easier to do this on paper than out in real life.

With the right kind of planning, you are going to be able to fit so much in a small area. Many people who are considering going with mini farming worry that they just won't have space to do more than just a small garden. But when you draw out the plans, you could have room for a small orchard, some chickens, a shed, and even a garden. Get some spray paint and outline the areas you will use for each part of the farm to see the visualization and to ensure everything goes where you would like.

Also, while you are doing your planning, make sure to check out some of the city ordinances. One difficult part about planning a mini farm in your backyard is that some city ordinances are not going to look fondly on some things like goats, chickens, and beehives in your backyard like they would if you were on an actual farm. Check into these things when making plans to make the best mini farm possible.

Location

The location of your plants and other items in the mini farm can really make a difference in the results that you see. You will want to make sure that you are placing your garden, orchards, and other plants in areas that are going to get quite a bit of sunlight. There is usually going to be someplace in the yard that gets the most sun, even if most of the yard is pretty shady, and this is where you should put the garden. On the other hand, you may want to leave your livestock inside areas that have more shade so they don't get overheated.

Another idea is to consider using supports that are found naturally in your yard. You can use trellises, fences, and other supports to help with plants with lots of vines. For example, tomatoes, peas, and runner beans will often be left in the garden to grow along the ground, but you can help them to grow up with the trellis to save space and use up more of the resources that you already have available.

Herbs

When working on your mini farm, don't forget to use some herbs. Herbs can be helpful in so many different ways. You can use them in your cooking to spice up the dishes that you like to eat, use them in your common household items, such as soaps, lotions, and more, and so much more. The best part is most of these are going to fit well right in between your other plants. In areas that are too small to add in more fruits or vegetables in the garden, herbs are going to fit in really well. They don't need a lot of sun so they can go under big and bushy plants and can grow in very small areas.

If your garden is already too full of items and you are worried about fitting in herbs, there are a lot of other places that you are able to grow the herbs that you would like. You can use an old wagon wheel and fill it with dirt and grow the herbs in there. Get some small containers and grow the herbs on a shelf inside your home. Hang them up in the air to keep them out of the way. There are so many different places where you can grow herbs to make life easier and to become even more self-sufficient.

Beehives

If you live in an area that allows it or you are out in the country, a beehive can be a great addition to your garden. You will get several benefits of using the beehives. First, the bees are going to be able to help with pollinating your flowers and plants so you will get a better yield than on your own. In addition, bees can be a great way to get some more food, including the honey that can taste so good in your kitchen. Choose to keep the honey or consider selling some to make a bit of extra money.

When raising bees in your backyard, you will need to take some special precautions to ensure that they are not feeling stressed out so they can do their jobs. This can be hard because you also need to keep them in the one area so you don't have to worry about the bees bothering your neighbors. While having bees can be a great addition to your farm, you do have to be careful before starting.

Chickens

One of the best things that you can do when starting your mini farm is bring in some chickens. Chickens are a lot of fun to raise, don't take a lot of work, can fit in a small backyard or on an acreage, and provide some healthy and fresh eggs and great meat. Raising chickens may seem a little bit hard at first, but you are going to love how easy the chickens can be.

To raise the chickens, you just need to make sure that you are getting things started right. Get some food that has many fantastic nutrients inside to help the chickens grow and find a coop that is big enough for them to grow and do well. Many families choose to allow the chickens to be free range and walk around the yard to destress the chickens and ensure that they aren't going to feel any unneeded stress.

You will need to take the time to check for eggs every day, watch for any diseases and illness that can sneak up on the chickens, and be sure that there isn't going to be issues with fighting between the chickens. You will have to be careful about cleaning out the chicken coops as well because the mess can cause issues if not properly taken care of. Consider selling some of the eggs, eating them, or allowing some to become fertilized so you won't have to worry about needing to purchase more eggs in the future.

Raising chickens is a great way to make sure that your family has plenty of fresh meat and eggs to stay healthy. The chickens don't take a lot of work as long as you let them take dirt baths and feed them each day and it can be a great way for your whole family to bond and enjoy time together. It doesn't matter if you have a big yard or a smaller one, chickens can be a great way to get started with mini farming.

Dairy

And finally, you are able to produce dairy products in your mini farm. While you are not going to be able to fit a whole cow or two in your backyard, but there are still others ways to include some more dairy in the mini farm. Small goats, such as the Australian Miniature

Goat, will not take up that much room inside of your backyard and while they do not produce the same amount of milk that the larger goat varieties do, they are better for your backyard space.

Goats are usually pretty easy to take care of. They have a laid back personality and won't take too much work to keep them happy. You will need to learn how to take care of the unique personality of your goat, but for the most part, if you feed them the right food and allow them a bit of room to roam around, they are going to produce the milk and dairy products that you are looking for.

Mini farming can be a great experience for the whole family to enjoy. It is a way to gain some of your own self-sufficiency from the modern world, get your hands nice and dirty, and to just enjoy some fresh produce and livestock even in your own backyard!

Chapter 2: Simple Tricks to Maximize Your Space

One of the hardest things for people new to this lifestyle to learn is how to make the most out of their space. They want to be able to do it all, but are worried that their backyard space may not be enough to get it done. If you are ready to be part of the mini farm movement and want to know how to fit as much stuff as possible into a little space, here are some great tips to help you get started.

Make a plan

Make a plan right from the beginning. Draw out what your backyard looks like and then separate into the different areas you would like to have. Consider how much space you will actually need for your goals. For example, a group of twenty chickens is most likely not going to fit in the smallest corner of your backyard as they will need some room to grow and flourish. Figure out how much of each thing you will like to have and how much space each of them need and make the diagrams from there.

During the beginning stages, it is fine to experiment. You may have a lot of lines all over the place as you try to decide how much space you have, where will be the best places to put everything, and how this will all work together. You may even need to give up a few things to fit it all in, such as having ten chickens instead of twenty. But soon you will find the plans that work the best for you and your mini farm can take off!

Decide what is the most important

Before you get too far into the process of mini farming, you need to decide what is the most important to you on this adventure. Are you most interested in having a huge garden that will provide you with all the produce you will need throughout the year or would you be more interested in the fresh meat and eggs. While you may be able to fit a bit of both into your mini farm, you do need to keep space in mind. You may have to choose one over the other a little bit to make things work and if you don't decide what is the most important from the beginning, you could end up in some trouble.

Designing the garden

The garden is often the area you are going to spend the most time on. Most of the animals that you include in your mini farm will just need a little food and roaming space and they are fine. But your garden can take up a lot of space when you're not carful and can make it really hard to get everything that you want into the small space. Some of the ways that you can maximize your mini farm includes:

- Have walkways—this can help you to get in between the plants a little bit better. You may not want to go with the regular row style of garden because this is inefficient and won't allow you to keep as much in the garden as before so having those walkways can help you to get to the plants and helps to separate out everything that you are growing.

- Raised garden beds—these are a convenient and easy way to harvest the food. You will find that you can fit twice as much food in one area without a lot of work, it helps to make the garden look better, and you will be able to get to the crops a little bit easier.
- Add in some trellises—there are quite a few plants that like to grow upward. In a traditional garden, they may go to the sides along the ground, but this is valuable space that you could use for other things in a mini farm. You can instead make your own trellises, or use some that are already in the garden, and teach the plants how to grow up. There is a lot of upward space you aren't using for anything else so you can really help to add more to a small space.
- Use the fence—just like with the idea of using a trellis to grow the plants upward, you can also turn to the fence to grow plants upwards rather than on the ground. If you are sharing a fence with a neighbor, it is probably not a good idea to allow the plants to grow that way so install a few fences to make this happen.
- Garden and landscaping—if you learn how to make the garden look unique and as part of the landscaping, you will not feel like it is taking up as much space.

Use Cages

Most people will just get started on their garden and allow the plants to grow in any way that they please. While this may be the easiest, it is going to take up a lot of space. Rather than allowing the plants to just go whichever way they would like, consider growing them in cages. This helps to keep the plants in check and can allow for more room for other plants. Tomato cages work well for this and can be used on things such as peppers.

Different kinds of planting.

One type of planting to try out is companion planting. This is the practice of planting certain vegetables and herbs together because they are able to benefit each other in some way, such as weed control or pest control, and they can save space. For example, planning squashes, beans, and corn together can be this kind of planting or planting herbs in between rows of other plants can be a type of companion planting. Each of the plants are going to share a smaller space while helping each other out in the process, making you have more space in the garden while planting twice as much.

Another method that you can use is successive planting. With this you will grow one crop and then once that crop becomes more mature, you will plant another round in the same area. The mature plants will help to protect the younger ones as they grow, allowing you to get two crops in the same area and not having to wait as long to get that second crop.

Utilize your space

Every farm is going to be a bit different. You are going to have a backyard that is different than what others may be using. You need to look around your own space and see what you are able to do to save room without making things look to cluttered. You may find that the yard is already divided up in a way that makes gardening in one area easier than in another and some yards may just have to separate all of this out. Use what your garden has available and you will be just fine.

Chapter 3: Best Plants for Mini Farming

When starting your mini farm garden, you will want to make sure that you are finding the best plants that will fit into a small space. There are so many vegetable and fruit plants that you can choose from, but some will take a lot of space and makes your garden very inefficient. This chapter is going to spend some time talking about the best plants that you can add into your small garden so you can feed your family even on a limited space.

Tomatoes

The first plant that you should consider is tomatoes. There are a lot of great tomato varieties that you can go with from the traditional juicy tomatoes that are often seen in gardens and even little cherry tomatoes that will do well as vines and can go up your fence or trellis if you're really short on room. You will need to consider whether you would like to have the indeterminate or determinate variety. The indeterminate variety can often get to four feet and will spread out to three feet, making them really big and hard for your garden to handle. For the mini farm with limited space, it is better to go with the determinate variety that will often stay around 2 feet or less.

Bush Beans

Wax or green beans will actually grow really well in a small space, especially when added into the ground with some of the other produce listed in this chapter. You should plant them in areas that are about a square foot and then have them planted between 2 and 4 inches apart in every direction. This means that you should be able to fit around six feet of beans in one square foot. Once you have harvested the beans, you should have enough time to get in another crop in the exact same area that year so you are getting a lot of great produce that year.

Cucumbers

The traditional cucumbers are really viney and take up a lot of space in your garden. You may be wondering how these are going to work for such a small space. In reality, the traditional cucumbers are not a good idea if you're looking to save space unless you have a fence or a trellis that you can use in order to keep them all in their places. Luckily, there are bush variety of cucumbers that you can use that will take up very limited amount of space while still producing a crisp vegetable that you will love. You will find that just two or three of these bush cucumbers will be enough for the whole family and they barely take up any space at all. While the taste may be a little bit different compared to what you enjoyed with the typical cucumber plants, these can save some room and you are going to be impressed by the fresh taste and ease of growing these plants.

Greens

Greens are so healthy for the whole body and can provide you with all of the great nutrition that your body needs to stay healthy. The best greens to add to your garden are all of those that you may want to consider for a salad. Options like beets, Swiss chard, and spinach won't take up that much space in a small space. You will be able to choose to grow the greens by the square foot or in wide rows so it will work well no matter how you decide to set up your garden. When the plant starts to become too thick and is taking over the rest of the garden, it is time for you to clip some off and eat it so it's the perfect plant to keep on growing, won't take up space, and will provide you with food all season long.

Salad greens such as radish, salad greens, and lettuce are good for small areas as well. You can plant them in many different ways and they are going to mature really quickly so you can easily get a few crops into the season. You can either choose to clip off the ends and eat through the season or just replant and have a fresh new crop at any time. You can also tuck these into the rows between other plants, such as your cucumber and tomato plants, and not have to worry about it as much.

Other Fruits and Vegetables

While the products listed above may be some of the best to use in your mini farm because they can produce a lot of great food in a limited amount of space, that does not mean that you are not allowed to use some of your other favorite fruits and vegetables in the garden. Anything can work, from peas to beans to pumpkins, watermelon, strawberries and more. The whole point here is to ensure that you are coming up with the proper plan to make sure everything is going to fit in just one area.

You may have to get creative here. Some of your options, such as pumpkins and watermelon, can take up a lot of space in a garden and could limit how much you are going to be able to produce in that area. But if you try out a few ideas, such as caging in watermelon and pumpkins so they are only allowed to grow in a more limited amount of space and you choose to grow beans and other lengthy plants on trellises, you may be able to get everything to fit in one small area, even though some of the plants take up more space.

Nothing is off limits when it comes to your mini farm and the great garden that you can produce. The important thing is to just become aware of how much space that you will have to work with and try to use it as efficiently as possible. This can take a little preplanning and practice, but you are sure to get it all figured out for one of the best farms possible.

Herbs

Herbs are often forgotten when it comes to planting your mini farm, but they are going to do a great job for so many things. You will be able to grow herbs o help with many homemade remedies and even to add to your cooking each day for some extra flavor. These herbs don't take up much space and will do an amazing job in any garden. In fact, most herbs do not need a lot of sun either so tucking them into the rows between some of your favorite vegetables and fruits can really help to fit more into a limited space while still getting a lot of produce out of the process.

These are just some of the ideas that you can go with when it comes to creating your mini farm. There are so many fresh fruits and vegetables that you can go with and pretty much anything is going to work in the garden, as long as you plan things out and use some of the suggestions in the chapter above to utilize the space better. Whether you would like a garden full of fruits or one full of vegetables, you will be able to make a lot of things work as long as you plan it out and use the space that you have available.

Chapter 4: Picking the Right Soil, Pest Control, and Taking Care of Weeds

Picking out the fruits and vegetables that you would like to use on your mini farm can be a fun experience, but what should you do when it is time to plant them or after they are already growing strong? There is still a lot of work that you will need to take care of from picking out the right soil, keeping the pests at bay, and even taking care of the weeds. In this chapter, we will take some time to look over these important aspects of taking care of your garden to ensure you get the most out of all your work.

Soil Options

While you are working on your garden, you need to make sure that you are picking out a soil that is good for the plants. Many farmers will choose to just use the soil that is available in their area, but this could mean that your plants are missing out on some of the important nutrients that they need to stay healthy. Adding in some more nutrients or designing your own soil can help to ensure that the plants are going to do fine without as much worry.

If you are choosing to use the soil that is already available in your yard, it is time to get to work. You will need to move the soil around and till it a bit to allow some more oxygen to get in and to release some of the nutrients that are inside. There can be a lot of good in the soil that you have available already, but you will need to bring it out to see results.

You will also need to pick out a good pH tester. This is going to tell you what nutrients are present in which amounts. Sometimes the soil will be just fine and other times you may want to consider bringing in some more nutrients to make the soil perfect for the plants that you would like to grow. You can choose to mix in some premade potting soil or make your own compost, perhaps with the chickens or goats that you are also raising on your mini farm.

No matter what kind of soil you are using, you will need to check the pH levels on occasion. Some plants are going to take a lot of nutrients out of the soil and if you're not careful, you could end up without something that is important to your plants. Set up a regular schedule for checking the pH levels or any time that you notice that some of the plants are yellowing or aren't doing as well, it may be time to add some new nutrients.

Pre-making your soil is another way to go. You may find that making up soil with the right nutrients or adding in a lot of compost can ensure that all those nutrients are available right from the very beginning. This may take a bit of work on your part to organize, but if you want those fruits and vegetables to flourish, you will really appreciate this effort.

Any time that some of the nutrients begin to fall short in your garden, it is time to add in the nutrients. There are many products available, many of which can be added in along with your watering routine, so you can give your plants the nutrients they need to flourish in a mini farm.

Pest Control

Pest control is another option that you will need to take care of when it comes to your garden. Many people assume they can just use bug sprays or other pest control sprays to take care of their gardens, but if you're not careful, you may find that these chemicals are going to cause some harm to your beautiful garden. Because of some of these issues with traditional pest controls, many people are turning to organic options to help make their gardens look amazing while keeping those pests away. Some of the options that you can use to help with natural and organic pest control include:

- Floating row covers—these are a porous fiber that is white and see through but will act as a barrier to insects. They still allow the sunlight in though so your plants are going to get all of the great nutrition they need in that part. If you would like to extend your season a bit longer, there are heavier duty row covers that will help to keep the plants warm.

- Pheromone traps—many insects are going to produce pheromones, or powerful smells that are meant to lure the opposite sex. There are special bait traps that have these scents on them that will help to alert you when a certain pest is trying to move into the area, but they may not be the best at keeping the pests away.
- Sticky traps—these are a rigid material that will have some kind of sticky substance on them that is meant to capture the insects and keep them still. You have to keep the traps clean and as sticky as possible and it is best to hang them at plant height every few feet. The color will also attract different kinds of pests so keep this in mind. For example, yellow is good for leafhoppers, whiteflies, and fruit flies while white is better for plant bugs and flea beetles. Light blue is good for flower thrips and red spheres can be good for some flies.
- Insecticidal soap—this kind of soap is going to include a fatty acid that will dissolve onto the skin of the insects. The insect needs to come into contact with the soap while it is still in liquid form so you will need to spray it onto the pests as they are flying around. You can also test it on each plant to make sure that the plant will be fine with that spray around.
- Essential oils—these are often the most effective because they are going to scare away the pests without causing harm to the plants. There are a number of essential oils that have a

smell that is bad for the pests, but the oils are made out of herbs so they aren't an issue to your plants. Make sure to research which oils work the best with your particular pests to help avoid issues.

While traditional forms of pest control may seem like the best options to take care of your pests and will help you to keep the plants healthy, they can actually cause a lot of harm to the plant. You could be spraying harmful chemicals at the plants and making them sick and ensuring they don't do well. Try out an organic option of the pest control and you will see that it is much easier to keep those pests away without ruining all your hard work.

How to Take Care of Weeds

Weeds are a pain for anyone who has ever worked in a garden. The weeds can take over the garden in no time and you will have to keep up on them all of the time. Weeds can cause a variety of issues when it comes to your garden. First, they are going to be really unsightly to your garden because they take up a lot of space and can take away from the beautiful garden that you are growing.

The biggest issue with weeds though is that they are taking up a lot of nutritional value that the garden plants will need. While the weeds will pose no value to you on your mini farm, they are going to pose a lot of issues when it comes to the nutrient content in the soil. Your plants and the weeds are going to start competing for all of the nutrients that are in the soil, despite the fact that you didn't put the weeds there and want nothing to do with them. If you don't take care of the weeds and let them overtake the garden, your crops are going to start to fail and you will just be left with weeds no matter how hard you work.

The best thing that you can do for he health of your garden and to keep the crops growing healthy is to take care of those weeds. You should check on the garden at least a few times each week, seeing how well the plants are growing, checking if there are issues with pests, and then to also see if the weeds are starting to sprout up. If you start to notice that there are weeds all over the place, take care of them right away. You can pull them out at the roots, use a safe weed remover, or any other method that will get rid of the weeds, just make sure to take care of them right away.

Taking care of your garden can seem like a big task, but if you just keep up with all of the work it won't seem so bad. Pick out the right soil and check on the pH levels from the beginning, learn how to find all natural ways to keep pests away, and keep up on those weeds and you are going to have the best mini farming garden that you could ask for.

Chapter 5: What Livestock Do Well with Mini Farming?

While gardening is often the first step that you can take when it comes to mini farming because it is really easy to do, another option for those who have the room and ambition is to bring in some livestock. There are many different animals that can do well with this limited space and will still give you all of the great meat, milk, and eggs that you need to stay healthy and happy with your mini farm.

There are a few things that you will need to take care of when it comes to picking out your livestock. First, you have to remember that you are dealing with limited space. You will not be able to bring in cows, horses, and other big animals and you will also have to be careful about the size of your flock when dealing with this smaller farm size. But there are alternatives such as goats to get milk and any of the animals below to get the great meat that you would like.

Before you go out and purchase the different animals that strike your fancy, you will need to make sure that you make a good plan for the area. Figure out where you would like to place your shed, your garden, and where the animals are going to be allowed to go. You may have to add in a few new fences to keep all of the livestock in one place and to ensure that they are not getting into your garden and ruining your hard work. With a good plan, you will be able to see how much room is actually available and can ensure that you will fit as many animals into the area as possible without crowding anything.

There are several different types of animals that you can consider bringing on board for your mini farm. The choice you make will depend on what you are trying to get out of the animals. You may be interested in just getting meat while others are looking to get eggs, milk, or a combination of the three. Here we will look at some of the best options that you can use when creating your mini farm including chickens, pigs, goats, and rabbits.

Chickens

One of the first animals that people will go after when they get started with mini farming is chickens. Chickens are so easy to take care of and can provide you with some of the best fresh eggs and fresh meat possible that it is no wonder that you will add these into your mini farm. You can even allow a few of the chickens to fertilize and get more without having to pay to keep them coming without having to pay for anything else.

Chickens are pretty easy to take care of even in your backyard. They don't take up a lot of room and won't make a lot of noise that will annoy the neighbors. You will need to make sure that they have a coop available. This provides them with a safe place to sleep at night and stay away from predators as well as to lay their eggs. As long as you provide them with some high quality food every day and allow them to roam around during the day, there is very little that you will need to do to get all the great eggs and meat that you need.

You can also choose how many chickens you would like to have around your home. Some choose to have one rooster and ten to fifteen chickens around. This is plenty to get fertilized eggs and to keep some more chickens growing over the years. Others decide to not deal with the rooster and will have a small flock of hens. Hens are able to lay their own eggs without the rooster so if you're just interested in the meat and eggs, this can be one of the best ways.

Chickens are a great way to help your family bond and can provide a ton of meat and eggs for a very little amount of work. These are good animals to have around if you have younger children because they are really easy to take care of and like the attention from other people. Learn how to take care of your particular type of chicken and you will find that it is easier than ever to get your own meat and eggs every day.

Goats

Goats can be a great substitute for cows on a mini farm. They may not be able to produce the same amount of meat and the same quality of milk, but they do well in both arenas on their own and can fit into the smaller space that your mini farm is going to require. Goats are really intelligent backyard creatures to have and they really like to be around other people, making them good companions if you have some kids around who would like to help out.

If you pick out a good doe, you should be able to expect a gallon or so of milk each day for the three to four pounds of grain along with a few pounds of hay. If you have a few goats in your farm, you should be able to produce enough milk to make the whole family happy. Goats milk is going to be similar to what you find with cows' milk with the added benefit if fewer allergens. If there is someone in your family who doesn't do well with cows' milk, you may be surprised at how well they will do with goats' milk.

You can choose from a wide variety of goats to add to your farm but make sure to check out the ones that are also good for meat. The chevon meat is some of the best that you and your family to enjoy. The hides from these animals are also amazing to make your own jackets, vests, and rugs among other garments.

While the goat can be a great way to make some of your own household items and can be pretty easy to take care of, there are some drawbacks. First, if you would like to get some milk from the goats, you are going to have to milk them two times each day, every day, for a period of ten months until the lactation period is done.

This can be really hard for some people based on their other obligations and the goat may not be the best choice for them. You will also need to keep the goats penned in to one area to ensure they aren't running around and getting out since they like to roam. Since the goats like to make a lot of noise, they usually aren't going to work well for a mini farm that is in town.

Pigs

Pigs can provide some wonderful meat for your family to enjoy and they often like to eat your leftovers so feeding them can be easy. In fact, your pigs are going to enjoy having surplus eggs, roots, grains, garden greens and your kitchen scraps in order to grow into some delicious meat that you are sure to enjoy. They are even better than dogs at cleaning up all that mess that you don't feel like taking care of when it comes to food waste.

Pigs are not going to need very much room and it is pretty easy to raise a couple within a pen that is just 16 square feet as long as you start them in this area from an early age. If you are purchasing for your mini farm, you should consider purchasing the weanlings during the spring and then raising them throughout the summer to reach their market weight. With this method, you will not have to worry about the issues that come with newborn piglets and you can avoid the huge size and issues of those that reach over 400 pounds.

To take care of the pigs, you just need to make sure that you are keeping them well fed and watered, something that you are going to need to do twice each day. Clean out the manure as often as you need. Some people will just do it when the compost pile is getting a bit low but you can set up your own schedule to make sure it all works out properly.

Most pigs are not going to be able to jump over a fence that you put up, but they may try to find holes available in the bottom of the fence so make sure everything is in its proper places. Have the fence be sturdy and check it often for any holes or weak spots where the pigs may try to get out.

Pigs can be a little bit dirty and cause a little bit of noise, especially if they happen to get out of their pens. You may want to consider just keeping it down to one or two pigs around your home to start with or wait until you have a little more space in order to invite these animals into the mini farm. Overall, they are pretty easy to take care of as long as you provide them with enough food and the amount of meat you can get out of them is amazing.

Rabbits

Rabbits are another great choice that you can make when it comes to getting started on your mini farm. Rabbits are fairly quiet animals so you won't have to worry about them being noisy or disturbing the neighbors and they are pretty clean and easy to take care of compared to some of the other animals that you may come across. They are also really prolific so you will be able to get more rabbits from the original bunch without having to pay for any more along the way.

You will be able to keep your rabbits out in the open or even in an all-wire hutch. If the rabbits are kept in a hutch, you will need to make sure that you are cleaning out from the cage on a regular basis to prevent a bad smell and to keep the rabbits healthy. They don't really take that much energy to take care of; just a little bit of food, some grooming, and taking care of their living environment if you keep them in cages. For this little amount of work, you will not be disappointed in the amount of food that you can get out of rabbits.

Keep in mind that if you do go with rabbits that they need to have a safe place to stay at night. Rabbits are really easy for prey to go after and if you leave the rabbits out without protection, your whole flock will be gone in no time at all.

Sheep

Sheep can be a great option as long as you have a little bit of space out in the country for the mini farming. They may be too loud to keep inside of town and some city ordinances may not be too fond of keeping these sheep around. But if you have a small little piece of land out in the country a little bit, perhaps a small amount of grass for one or two sheep to graze, you will find that these can be the perfect addition to your work.

Sheep are pretty easy to take care of. You can raise them completely on good grassland, when it is in season, without having to add in any supplemental grains, making them one of the most economical creatures that you can take care of. Once the adult ewe is ready to harvest, you will get a good 100 pounds of meat as well as 8 pounds of wool from every one. This means that just having a small herd of four or five could be enough to keep your family fed for the winter. And if you go with some of the European varieties of sheep you can even get some milk out of your sheep flock.

The caretaking for sheep can be minimal as well. You will need to take care to shorn them each year, and this does pose some problems if you want to produce a good fleece for spinning and it does take some time and skill to learn. The equipment can be expensive to do this. If you want to have sheep on your mini farm, it may be best to hire a professional shearer to do the work for you. This can save you a lot of time and can keep costs down since you won't have to purchase all the supplies for yourself.

For those sheep who are lambing, you will need to spend some extra time with them. This helps to keep the ewes healthy during the pregnancies and can ensure that the ewes are going to be assisted during labor and do a good job of watching after their lambs properly after birth. You will also have to spend some special time watching the sheep as they are very timid and many predators like to go after them as easy prey.

No Cows

As nice as it would be to have some cows running around your farm, both for the delicious and fresh milk and for the great tasting meat, it is unlikely that you will have the room that is necessary to keep a heard of cows on your small little farm. While you may have up to ¼ of an acre to be a mini farm, most cows are going to need a lot more room and for each cow that you want to add to the herd, you are going to need a bit more room.

So when it comes to mini farming, you are going to have to leave the idea of cows behind because there is simply not the room to make it happen. You won't have the room to allow the cows to roam around, you won't have the room to store them, it will be difficult to keep enough food and grass around to make the cows happy, and the amount of manure that the cows will bring about can quickly overpower your small area.

You will also need to be careful with other big animals. While some of the bigger animals, such as cows, horses, and larger herds of the smaller animals, may fit well on a regular farm, you need to remember that you are a bit more limited on space and need to go with some of the smaller varieties. With a little bit of adjusting and hard work, you will be able to get all the products that you need in the smaller space.

Luckily, there are other options that you can choose when it comes to getting the products that you might miss from the cows. You can raise chicken, sheep, pigs and more to get some of that great fresh meat that you want. It may not be the same as fresh beef, but they are much easier to fit into a small area and can work great for providing food for the family. In addition, goats are perfect for providing your family with some fresh milk if that's what you're looking for and with some of the miniature varieties, you may be able to fit a whole herd into your mini farm.

Chapter 6: Tips to Make Mini Farming Easier

Getting started on mini farming can seem like a monumental task. You may be excited to get started on every aspect of mini farming and want to fit in as much stuff in one area as possible, but you are limited by space and most likely your time. When you are ready to try out mini farming and are worried about how to get started, follow some of these great tips:

- Use the space you have—everyone comes to mini farming with a different amount of space. Some may have a larger area of up to ¼ an acre and others are dealing with a tiny backyard in the middle of town. But no matter how small of space you are dealing with, you can still enjoy this kind of farming. Learn how to use the space that you have; a small space is all you need for a garden or maybe decide to leave the chickens outside and do some indoor growing if you don't have the space. Everyone has some space and you can make it work!
- Try something new—don't be afraid of trying something new when it comes to this kind of farming. You may not be a fan of gardening, but wouldn't it be kind of cool to have some chickens to take care of and get fresh eggs in the morning? Are you interested in bringing a goat or two into your

backyard? Don't be scared to try out something new; you might be surprised at how much fun it can be.

- Start out with one thing—if you have never done anything with homesteading or farming in the past, start out with one thing. Perhaps try out a garden in the first year and grow just a handful of plants. This helps you to get your feet wet without taking on more than you can handle in the beginning.
- Realize you have more space than you think—many people who don't have a big acreage assume they don't have enough space to do any kind of farming. But you really have more space than you think if you look around. Consider that you just need a small corner of your backyard to make a garden and chickens do well in a little area the size of a small shed. If you are willing to give up a little bit of your backyard, you can get started on your mini farm.
- You don't have to do it all—we discuss a lot of different things when it comes to mini farming and it may all seem a bit overwhelming. Remember that you do not have to try all of it at once. Perhaps you just want to get started with a garden or you want to keep some chickens in your backyard. These can all be a part of mini farming even if you don't do them all together. Pick one or two things to do if you're overwhelmed and you will find it is easier to do well with this farming.
- Enlist others to help—sometimes getting started on a farm, even a smaller one, can be scary. There are so many things

that you will need to keep in line and you may not know everything. For example, you may have no idea how to pick out goats and to raise them. Asking others to help out, either experts in the area you are exploring or others you know who are starting mini farming, can really make this easier and helps your mini farm to be a success.

- Have fun—the most important thing that you should remember when it comes to starting your mini farm is that it should be fun. Yes you are going to have a lot of work to do, the amount will depend on how much you decide to do with this process. But if you're not having fun, perhaps mini farming is not the right choice for you to make. But if you work hard and try a few different things in the process, you will find that mini farming does not have to be such a challenge and can actually be a lot of fun.

Mini farming is an experience that the whole family can enjoy. You can have a combination of growing a garden, having an orchard, and even taking care of chickens. Whether you have younger children or older, there is something for everyone to enjoy when it comes to farming, even in a limited space. Don't let your lack of a large acreage keep you away from having a lot of fun with farming and reaching your own self-sufficiency, learn about mini farming and have so much fun along the way.

Conclusion

Many people have gotten into the idea that it is better to gain some sort of self-sufficiency. They may be tired of all the dependency that they are dealing with in the modern world and worried about what will happen if things start to go south. Others may love the idea of starting their own farm but aren't able to afford or find a nice acreage in their area that allows them to follow this dream. Mini farming could be the best way to reach these goals without having to go all out or worry about not having enough land.

Anyone is able to participate in mini farming. As long as you are able to start a small garden or take care of a few animals for food, or a combination of it all, you can get started on mini farming. Doing all of this work may seem like it is impossible to do, but you can start out slowly and soon you will see that it is a lot of fun and something that you can totally handle.

This guidebook is meant to provide you with all of the information and tips that you need in order to do well with mini farming. Whether you have been into the whole homesteading movement or enjoyed some self-sufficiency in the past or you are completely new to the project, you may enjoy the life of mini farming. Look through this guidebook and learn everything that you need to do well with mini farming no matter what space you have available.

Printed in Poland
by Amazon Fulfillment
Poland Sp. z o.o., Wrocław